The Workings of Human Rights, Law, and Justice

A Journey from Nepal to Nobel Nominee

I0885345

Surya P. Subedi

QC (Hon), OBE, DCL & DPhil (Oxford)

Professor of International Law, University of Leeds, United Kingdom; Former UN Special Rapporteur for Human Rights in Cambodia; Barrister, Three Stone Chambers, Lincoln's Inn, London

Routledge
Taylor & Francis Group
LONDON AND NEW YORK

First published 2022
by Routledge
4 Park Square, Milton Park, Abingdon, Oxon OX14 4RN

and by Routledge
605 Third Avenue, New York, NY 10158

Routledge is an imprint of the Taylor & Francis Group, an informa business

British Library Cataloguing-in-Publication Data
A catalogue record for this book is available from the British Library

Library of Congress Cataloging-in-Publication Data
A catalog record has been requested for this book

ISBN: 978-1-032-22196-0 (hbk)
ISBN: 978-1-032-22203-5 (pbk)
ISBN: 978-1-003-27154-3 (ebk)

DOI: 10.4324/9781003271543

Typeset in Galliard
by Deanta Global Publishing Services, Chennai, India

The Workings of Human Rights, Law, and Justice

Drawing on the personal experience of a leading international jurist, this book provides insights into the workings of international law and human rights from a global perspective.

The work follows the author's remarkable journey from a simple village in Nepal to becoming an international jurist acclaimed for his innovative academic and influential practical legal work and nomination for the Nobel Peace Prize. It offers insights into the powers bearing on international policymaking, the dynamics of human rights negotiations with governments, and the effects of their outcomes on the lives of their citizens. While much has been written on international human rights law, this inspirational memoir casts a new light on the working of human rights, law, and justice through the eyes of a leading actor. It provides a valuable contribution to the study of justice and human rights and the importance of individual action. As such, the book presents an accessible source for current debates around the development and effectiveness of international law and human rights and practices for decolonising these debates.

The book will provide inspiration and practical guidance for students, academics, international lawyers, jurists, and human rights advocates.

Surya P. Subedi QC is Professor of International Law at the University of Leeds, UK, and a Barrister at Three Stone Chambers, Lincoln's Inn, London. He has served as the UN special rapporteur for human rights in Cambodia, as an adviser on human rights to the British foreign secretary, and as legal procedural adviser to the World Conservation Congress of the International Union for Conservation of Nature. He holds a DPhil and a DCL from the University of Oxford. He was elected to the Institut de Droit International in 2011. He has acted as a counsel in several cases before the International Court of Justice.

Routledge Research in Human Rights Law

Hate Speech and Human Rights in Eastern Europe
Legislating for Divergent Values
Viera Pejchal

Collective Punishment and Human Rights Law
Addressing Gaps in International Law
Cornelia Klocker

Executive Clemency
Comparative and Empirical Perspectives
Edited by Daniel Pascoe and Andrew Novak

International Human Rights Law and Crimes Against Women in Turkey
Legislation on So-Called Honour Killings
Ayşe Güneş

Rights of the Child, Mothers and Sentencing
The Case of Kenya
Alice Wambui Macharia

Capturing Caste in Law
The Legal Regulation of Caste Discrimination
Annapurna Waughray

The Workings of Human Rights, Law, and Justice
A Journey from Nepal to Nobel Nominee
Surya P Subedi, QC

For more information about this series, please visit:
www.routledge.com/Routledge-Research-in-Human-Rights-Law/book-series/HUMRIGHTSLAW

Dedicated to

All Human Rights Defenders Around the Globe

Contents

Plates/Photos

Foreword

This foreword marks the beginning of a long journey and acquaintance that neither Surya nor I could have ever foreseen. I can vividly remember our days as doctoral students at Oxford in the early 1990s: both Surya and I studied international law, taking our first steps on a path that would take each of us further afield and ever deeper into the world of international law and human rights scholarship, international law-making, and the intricacies of its application worldwide. In the years since, Surya and I have collaborated on international human rights projects; participated in the Advisory Group on Human Rights to the British foreign secretary; served as UN special rapporteurs for human rights. I am proud to say that Surya has become a foremost distinguished international lawyer both in theory and in practice.

From the outset, I especially respected Surya for his adventurous, action-oriented approach in fiercely challenging wrongdoing, while creating space for dignity and respect towards the people involved. His outstanding and respected work in Cambodia and Nepal, which he recounts in this book, is a case in point. Rather than harshly criticising people who cause harm, Surya focuses on the harm itself and on preventing the behaviours that cause it. He establishes a connection with all stakeholders, securing the cooperation which is a prerequisite for shared, decisive action towards changing the circumstances and actions that cause hardship.

Surya embraces a culture of accountability and a victim-centred approach to countering impunity, and understands how to bring people in. His ethos is a significant departure from traditional 'blame and shame' practices, whereby individuals, organisations, and state representatives are confronted with their failings, and are thus forced into an adversarial position. Such encounters bear the hallmarks of a hostile battle and thus almost inevitably prove futile. Surya's successful approach to human rights work is one of productive conversations and advocacy for clear legal responsibilities. This memoir offers examples of his transformative engagement with individuals from all walks of life and state officials in conflict situations, which renders it a refreshing, timely read.

I am honoured to write this foreword to Surya's memoir, which is imbued with the spirit and enthusiasm of a man devoted to the promotion of the rule of law, democracy, and human rights. Surya is credited for developing the concept of a zone of peace (ZOP) in international law. Deeply influenced since childhood by the eastern philosophies of peace and non-violence enshrined in the Vedic and Buddhist scriptures, Surya dedicated his doctoral thesis to the study of the principles underlying the concept of a ZOP in international law. Convinced that development and human rights are necessary prerequisites for peace, as enshrined in the 1945 United Nations Charter, Surya has devoted himself to these causes. He tackles challenges by employing both his rigorous academic insight and his international advocacy by means of applied legal skills; and in doing so, has charted a path of truly transformational work.

In promoting human rights globally, Surya has engaged in the academic study of human rights policy and practice, as well as in hands-on legal action. His work has been recognised both by governments and by pre-eminent global and national institutions.

In April 2021, the flagship magazine of the Bar Council of England published a feature article on Surya, entitled 'The International Human Rights Jurist', which captures the essence of a lifetime spent promoting and protecting human rights. In a way, this book is an extended version of that story, which merits wide retelling and makes for gripping reading. Surya's remarkable tale deserves to be known from Nepal to the United Kingdom and beyond. His personal journey and achievements in academia, the legal profession, and the UN make this book a valuable resource for all. It should be of interest not only to an international legal and human rights audience, but also to a broader readership in international relations, diplomacy, legal sociology, legal anthropology and generally as an autobiography or memoir, since the content has universal appeal. I hope that readers will likewise find this book engaging, interesting, uplifting, and illuminating.

Professor Chaloka Beyani, DPhil (Oxford)
London School of Economics and Political Science (LSE)
Member of the UK Foreign Secretary's Advisory Group on Human Rights; Former UN special rapporteur on the human rights of internally displaced persons 2010–2016

Preface

Many people who know me, my background, and my contribution to international law and human rights have urged me to write a memoir for some time now. The first to do so were my colleagues in the United Nations, when I completed my UN mandate in Cambodia. I received similar encouragement from my colleagues at the University of Oxford after I was awarded its highest accolade – the Doctor of Civil Law – in 2019. Other friends and colleagues who kept nudging me in this direction included Professor Michael Cardwell at the University of Leeds, who observed: 'Not everybody has as many interesting experiences to share with the wider public as you have'.

In my view, a memoir is essentially a historical account or biography written from personal experience. It is a book about an individual's life, notable contributions to society, lessons learned, and defining moments – and this is the template I have followed in this memoir. In writing it, I have drawn on anecdotes from my life relating to my work in international law and human rights. Therefore, this volume is basically a professional memoir that recounts my experiences as an international law and human rights academic, as a practitioner in the field, and as a senior UN official. As Oscar Wilde said, 'Experience is the name everyone gives to their mistakes'.[1] Thus, this volume naturally reflects not only my successes in my field, but also my near-misses and failures.

Former US President Richard Nixon explained in his memoirs that he had a habit of making extensive handwritten notes about his ideas, conversations, activities, and speeches on yellow legal notepads, extending to more than 20,000 pages in total.[2] Although I am a bird

1 Oscar Wilde, *Lady Windermere's Fan* (1892), Mr. Dumby, Act III. Methuen Drama, London.

2 Richard Nixon, *The Memoirs of Richard Nixon* (Sidgwick & Jackson, London, 1978), p ix.

of a rather different feather, I too have always had a habit of jotting down my ideas (big and small), experiences, and activities on pieces of paper – mostly on Post-it notes. My family members are all too familiar with the scene of my study desk festooned with piles and piles of Post-its – albeit in a certain order – and folder after folder of papers about my lifetime experiences.

I have also kept an annual diary since I became a full professor of law at the University of Hull in 1999. That was also the year that I first went to New York to teach at a law school as a visiting professor. The law school provided me with a beautiful apartment in a high-rise building in Brooklyn Heights. My family accompanied me on this trip; and upon seeing the view from the window of our apartment for the first time, my wife Kokila remarked on the picture-perfect panorama of lower Manhattan and the bay into which the Hudson and East Rivers converge. I wanted to capture that memorable moment in time and started keeping a diary thenceforth. In the period between Christmas and New Year, I made a habit of reviewing the year gone by – with the help of my Post-it notes – and writing up an annual diary, reflecting on the major events that had transpired in our personal and family lives. When I sat down to write this memoir, my Post-its and diaries proved invaluable.

I would like to take this opportunity to pay my tribute to my late father, Pandit Hom Nath, and my late mother, Tuka Devi, for their love and guidance, and for providing me with a wonderful environment in which to grow and learn during the early years of my life. I am also most grateful to my three elder brothers – Komal Nath, Devi Prasad, and Dhruba Prasad – for their love, guidance, and support throughout my life. I also would like to pay tribute to the late King Birendra of Nepal and Professor Sir Ian Brownlie of the University of Oxford, who were instrumental in the early days of my academic career. My sincere thanks also go to Professor Jo Carby-Hall, Professor Christine Gray, Sir Adam Roberts, Judge Sir Christopher Greenwood, Ambassador Christopher Pinto, Professor Nico Schrijver, Professor David Freestone, Professor Scott Davidson, and Professor Clive Walker, for their assistance and guidance throughout my career.

I am most grateful to Professor Chaloka Beyani of the London School of Economics and Political Science, for writing the foreword to this memoir. Among many others to whom I would like to record my gratitude are Dr Ali Abusedra, for his steadfast allegiance over many years and for sharing his perspectives on life with me; Dr James Busuttil, for his friendship and numerous acts of kindness; Mr Richard Nowinski, Dr Harsha Singh, Professor Nigel White, Professor Chris Bovis, Professor

Kim Van der Borght, Sir Malcolm Evans, Professor Michael Cardwell, Professor Steven Wheatley, Professor Graham Dutfield, Professor Sienho Yee, Professor Simon Chesterman, Professor Antony Anghie, Dr Tan Hsien-Li, Dr Mavluda Sattarova, Professor David Gellner, Professor Michael Hutt, Professor B.S. Chimni, Professor Yogesh Tyagi, Professor Bharat Desai, Professor Javaid Rehman, Professor Upendra Acharya, Professor Padam Simkhada, Justice Dr Anand Mohan Bhattarai, Justice Sapana Malla, Justice Hari Phuyal, Lawrence Martin, Constantinos Salonidis, Khagendra Chhetry, Professor Bipin Adhikari, Professor D.N. Parajuli, Professor Saroj Krishna Ghimire, Dr Anirudhha Rajput, Dr Krishna Adhikari, Dr Nicolette Butler, Dr Amrita Mukherjee, Dr James Watson, Dr Louisa Ashley, Dr Pratyush Nath Upreti, Dr Amrisha Pandey, and Dr Punam Yadav, for their intellectual collaboration; Dr Steven Turner, Andrew Stuart, and Andre Tilleman, for their camaraderie – especially as members of our hiking group over so many years; Tom and Linda Veblen, Professor Louise Ellison, Ambassador Andrew Sparks, Ambassador Durga Bahadur Subedi, Dr Raghav Dhital, Dr Gillian Holdsworth, Dr Hilary Christie, Amanda Hemingway, and Tracey Rogers, for their warmth and support; and Ambassador Dr Dinesh Bhattarai, Ambassador Dr Arjun Karki, Foreign Secretary Bharat Raj Paudyal, Dr Rajan Bhattarai, Dr Upendra Mahato, Kul Chandra Gautam, Jiba Lamichhane, Kul Acharya, Ram Sharan Simkhada, Bhagirath Yogi, Nabin Pokharel, Surendra Shrestha, Devendra Shrestha, and Dhruba Aryal, for their friendship.

My sincere thanks also go to Carolyn Boyle, for her superb assistance with this manuscript; and to Senior Commissioning Editor Alison Kirk and her team at Routledge, for their immensely helpful and efficient work. I am also grateful to Routledge's three external reviewers for their constructive comments on the manuscript.

Finally, I thank Kokila, my devoted partner during our 33-year journey together; Mevrouw Usha, for her insight and encouragement; Rajesh and Susana, Srijana and Vinod, Abhinav and Kanchan, Dinesh and Sushmita, Induka and Hari, Pranay, Anita, and Lucia, for their love and support.

Surya P. Subedi
London, 15 January 2022

About the Author and the Book

Professor Surya P. Subedi ranks among an exceptional group of international human rights jurists who have served in high-level positions in national and international organisations and governments with responsibility for policy formulation and advice. Over a long and varied career in the field of international law and human rights, he has extended the frontiers of knowledge in international law and human rights; influenced developments in law and policy in these areas; taught at several prestigious universities around the globe; and practised as an advocate and barrister in these areas of law. Very few international jurists can have touched the lives of so many people as profoundly as Professor Subedi. He has worked tirelessly to encourage and assist governments in working towards establishing independent judiciaries and in upholding human rights.

As a highly regarded professor of international law in Britain today, Professor Subedi has made a vital contribution to the development of international law and the advancement of human rights. His publications have inspired academic debate, set research agendas, and led to reform in international human rights law and global institutions. His research has engaged a range of audiences beyond academia – intellectuals, politicians, and diplomats involved with international law and human rights – and has informed their thinking and actions.

During his tenure as UN special rapporteur for human rights in Cambodia, he secured the release of journalists from prison, facilitated the safe return of the exiled opposition leader, improved prison conditions, and modified land concessions to mitigate human rights abuses in the then strife-torn country. He also has served as the adviser on human rights to the British foreign secretary and assisted the Nepalese government in drafting a new democratic constitution after the political upheavals brought about by the Maoist insurgency in the country;

and has been engaged in high-profile cases before international courts and tribunals.

Professor Subedi's contribution to human rights and justice has been recognised by the award of highly coveted accolades such as QC, OBE, and DCL, and the nomination for the Nobel Peace Prize and for UN High Commissioner for Human Rights. In this memoir, he traces his journey from humble beginnings in a small Nepalese village, where he was imbued with the values of learning and knowledge and the advancement of the greater good, to become an international jurist acclaimed for his innovative academic and influential practical legal work and for his meritorious accomplishments.

The book offers insights into the powers that bear on international policymaking, the dynamics of human rights negotiations with governments, and the effects of their outcomes on citizens' lives. It is an empowering narrative offering a story of complex experiences and perspectives where individual commitment and advocacy makes a real difference to our world. It provides rare glimpses of a personal journey and a life lived in law and the pursuit of justice and an insight into the workings of international law and international institutions through the eyes of an expert who has navigated the system and has been able to achieve meaningful and impactful outcomes. It gives hope and inspiration for future generations that individual action is meaningful despite the trials and tribulations inherent in life.

The author on a UN human rights mission in Cambodia in 2010

1 The Himalayan Life

From Rebel Leader to Royal Adviser

The Journey of My Ancestors

Much of human civilisation has evolved through migration, and my own ancestry is no different. The latest scientific thinking suggests that human beings originated in the Zambezi river valley, moved north through the African continent, and crossed over to the Eurasian landmass. By the time they arrived in the Sumerian region, human society and culture – language, script, and art – had become increasingly advanced. The civilisation that developed around the Sumerian region gradually spread to the east, west, north, and south. Those who headed east of the modern-day Caspian Sea and eventually settled in the Eurasian region are likely to have been my early ancestors.

They were the Vedic people – the composers and followers of the Vedas. During their migration from the Hindu Kush through the Khyber Pass into the Indus Valley, they documented in the Vedic scriptures the names of places and rivers in Iran and Central and West Asia. During their long journey to South Asia, they seem to have adopted and adapted to some of the local cultures they encountered, and they incorporated aspects of these cultures into the Vedas and other scriptures when refining them upon arriving in the modern-day Punjab area. For example, the Hindu and Buddhist scriptures refer to and glorify the Meru or Sumerian mountains. This reference likely points to an area in Mesopotamia – a historical region of Western Asia situated within the Tigris–Euphrates river system, in the northern part of the Fertile Crescent.

Moving eastwards via Iran (there are many similarities between the ancient Iranian religion of Zoroastrianism and the Vedic religion) and Afghanistan, the Vedic people eventually reached the Indus Valley,

DOI: 10.4324/9781003271543-1

which is located in modern-day Punjab. The name 'Punjab' is derived from the Sanskrit word 'panch aap' ('five rivers'), meaning 'the area blessed by five rivers'. The Vedic people living in this area were referred to as 'Indoos' by foreigners, especially the ancient Greeks and Romans. This term was soon used to refer to the people living in and around the Indus (Sindhu) river basin. Over time, phonetic changes to the term 'Indoos' gradually resulted in the modern-day term 'Hindus'. However, the Hindus called themselves 'Aryans', to signify their origins in the Caspian Sea region and distinguish themselves from the indigenous peoples of South Asia.

Continuing their journey eastwards, my ancestors crossed the Sutlej – a tributary of the Indus river – and continued via the foothills of the Himalayas in the upper reaches of several rivers, all originating in the Himalayas. Moving further east, from the Indus Valley through the foothills of the Himalayas, the Aryans settled in the fertile plains of the Ganges and Yamuna rivers, where their society flourished. It is here that the great and timeless epics of the Ramayana and Mahabharata were composed. The vast area between the Indus river to the west, the Brahmaputra river to the east, the Vindhya mountains to the south, and the majestic Himalayas to the north thus became the cradle of the Hindu civilisation.

The Brahmins of Varanasi

My ancestors – known as the Brahmins of Varanasi – settled in and around the ancient city of Varanasi (also known as the 'Athens of the East', due to its importance as a centre of knowledge and culture) for hundreds of years, where they engaged in learning the scriptures, expanding and expounding on them, and practising their Vedic beliefs. However, they subsequently came under attack during the Mughal rule. During the reign of Aurangzeb, they were even threatened with forcible conversion to the religion of the Mughals. India had long been admired and envied for its ancient civilisations and its thriving economy and culture, and was also one of the most populous nations in the world. As a result, it attracted the attentions of various conquering foreign rulers – such as the Turks, the Mongols, the Arabs, and the Mughals – which all invaded and colonised the country prior to the arrival of the British as new colonial rulers of India.

In the late seventeenth century, during the Mughal rule, my ancestors – fearing the impending assault on their way of life by Aurangzeb's advancing army[1] – migrated towards the Himalaya mountains in search of a new life. They initially settled in the Karnali river basin and then moved further eastwards to the Gandaki river basin. They flourished in the fertile valleys of the Ganges and its tributaries in Nepal, which flow from their source in the Himalayas through the northern Indian plains and empty into the Bay of Bengal. Benefiting from the rich alluvial soil of the snow-fed rivers for growing food, these valleys became central hubs of literature, art, and culture. The Hindu-Aryan civilisation reached its pinnacle here, generating new ideas and philosophies as reflected in the scriptures of Hinduism, Buddhism, and Jainism, and of various Hindu sects, such as the Vaishnav and Shaiva sects.

It was also in this geographically remote yet culturally rich area of Nepal – in a picturesque village known as Lamjung Khudi, located in the foothills of the Himalayas within the Annapurna mountain range – that I was born on 23 January 1958, on a frosty, sunny morning.

Life in the Annapurna Mountain Range

Nestled in the foothills of the Himalayas – a region hitherto inhabited by indigenous mountain peoples – my ancestors had continued in their profession of Brahmins, learning and preserving the Vedic scriptures, and teaching the Vedic values. I was initiated into this tradition myself at the tender age of seven, in a ceremony in which I promised to live by Vedic values. The initiation ceremony marks the start of a process in which one's third eye is activated, enabling one to see things that one's physical eyes cannot. It is the beginning of a journey towards spiritualism, enlightenment, and fulfilment in life. In the initiation ceremony, a boy gains the status of a Brahmin or 'twice-born', pledges to uphold Vedic values and embarks on the road to education, in order to become an educator himself eventually. Having undergone these rituals, one is supposed to lead a regimented life, filled with Brahmin duties and obligations. The ceremony also marks the start of formal schooling and indoctrination into the Hindu way of life.

As the tradition then dictated, I attended a Sanskrit school. My father, Pandit Hom Nath, was a teacher in the only Sanskrit school in

1 See John Keay, *India – A History: From the Earliest Civilisations to the Boom of the Twenty-First Century* (Harper Press, London, 2010), pp 342–3.

the area and my granduncle – Pandit Badri Nath, a revered Sanskritist – was the headmaster. The medium of instruction was mostly Sanskrit, with some Nepali, the country's official language. When I topped the class in grade 4, the headmaster decided to move me directly into grade 6, assuming that I would be able to cover the material for both grades 5 and 6 that year. When I outperformed my classmates in grade 6 too, I was admitted straight to grade 8. I came first again in the grade 8 examinations and also passed the Pratham Parixa in Sanskrit – the first qualification that a Brahmin boy from a traditional academic family was expected to obtain in Nepal at the start of his journey in life. This was as far as I could go at that school.

Having graduated from the Sanskrit school, I joined a recently established mainstream Nepali upper secondary school and started learning the English alphabet at the age of 13, while preparing for my first state exam, the School Leaving Certificate Examination (SLCE). In Nepal, this exam is regarded as the gateway to further education, as well as to any meaningful employment in life. At this school, I was made captain of the volleyball team (it was not possible to play football in this hilly region, due to the lack of a sufficiently large flat area for a pitch); and was subsequently elected president of the school students' union.

My life in this village, tucked away in the foothills of the Annapurna mountain range, was as blissful as one could imagine. We were 'organic' children and our lives were all organic – so much so that rice with fresh milk, both from our own farm, tasted like rice pudding without any need to add sugar. Rice and milk were the main components of our staple diet. Sadly, since the introduction of modern farming methods, the rice these days has lost its richness and fragrance. I often yearn for this old life, but it no longer exists: modernity has invaded even such remote areas of Nepal and it is no longer possible to enjoy the same quality of life.

The Wisdom of the East that Shaped My Life

I was the youngest son in a family of ten siblings, and our whole village was inhabited exclusively by Subedis, who followed the religious prescriptions as strictly as possible. The traditional Sanskrit education that I received in my formative years had a profound impact on me, and the moral and ethical values that I learned during my school years continue to guide me to this day. Traditionally, Brahmins focus on enhancing their intellectuality rather than on worshipping a deity. My initiation ceremony at the age of seven was my introduction and induction into Brahminhood. My life began to be guided by high moral and ethical values according to which I was to become an example of virtue in society, continually enhance my intellectuality, and gain as much education as possible so that I would one day be in a position to educate others.

The main purpose of my initiation ceremony was to receive a sacred mantra, known as the Gayatrti mantra, from a guru. According to tradition, this guru could be one's own father if he himself was a learned person; alternatively, he could be a close senior family member, if he enjoyed the status of a learned man in society, or a family priest. I received the sacred mantra from my father, as he himself was a scholar of Sanskrit, a schoolteacher, and a priest, and was thus eminently qualified to give the mantra to a young boy.

The Gayatri mantra reads as follows:

> I take refuge in Ric, the Word; I take refuge in Yajus, the Mind; I take refuge in Saman, the Breath; I take refuge in sight and hearing … [Therefore,] Earth, Ether, Heaven! The adorable glory of Savitar, the god of intellect, we contemplate; May he arouse our intellect.

The Vedas command a young boy to strive by thought, word, and deed towards the attainment of wellbeing for all living things. Having received the mantra from the guru, he must meditate every day, focusing on the message in the prayers. Thus, yoga, meditation, and prayers for the wellbeing of humanity became compulsory activities for me from the age of seven. I have performed these practices every morning throughout my life; they lift my spirits and energise me for the day ahead. I have found it immensely therapeutic to chant the ancient mantras handed down from generation to generation since time immemorial and to recite some verses from the Bhagvad Gita and Shrimad Bhagavatam every morning.

The Sanskrit education of my early school years focused on learning the ancient Vedic scriptures and the moral and ethical values prescribed for an orderly society. We were taught that it was our duty to treat our parents, female family members, and other members of society in general with respect. In the society in which I grew up, one's parents were considered next to God in the hierarchy of respect, followed by one's teachers. Parents and teachers were worshipped, both metaphorically and literally – female members of the family were given the name 'Devi' as a middle name to signify that they embodied the qualities of a goddess.

For example, after becoming a parent, a husband was duty-bound to pay his wife the same respect he paid to his own mother. The associated Sanskrit verse reads: 'matribat putra mataram'. A different verse reads: 'Rajpatni guropanti mitrapatni tathaiba cha panti mata swamata cha panchaita matar smrita', meaning that a man is obliged to treat the wife of the king, the wife of his teacher, the wife of his friend, and the mother of his wife as he treats his own mother. And the verse 'Matribat para dareshu, paradrabyeshu losthabat' states that one should treat the wife of another man the way one treats one's own mother, and the wealth of other men with indifference.

Education is another key value in the Sanskrit verses. Education is extolled as the best form of wealth that one can earn: it cannot be stolen by a thief or taken away by the king (or the state) in tax; nor does one need to divide it among one's siblings; nor is it heavy to carry. It is a form of wealth that keeps increasing even as you spend it. This emphasis on education is also expressed in the African proverb: 'Knowledge is better than wealth: you have to look after the wealth, but knowledge looks after you'.

At the same time, the Sanskrit verses stipulate that we must be both selective and intentional in gaining knowledge and education. This is because there is an abundance of books and areas of study available, but our time is limited and we face many hurdles in our lives. Therefore, as the Nepalese proverb says, we must do what a swan would do when separating milk from water: take the milk and leave the water. As scholars, we were not to be in the habit of accumulating wealth or seeking material satisfaction; our duty was to research, learn, and advance knowledge.

It was made clear to us from the outset that those who pursued material happiness would gain little knowledge and those who pursued knowledge would gain little material wealth. The rewards of our intellectual pursuits, however, would be immensely satisfying. One Sanskrit verse states that there can be no comparison between the ruling classes and learned people; the ruling classes are respected only in their country, while learned people are respected worldwide. We were told that no decoration that can be placed on our body is greater than knowledge. Knowledge is what we should all seek and aspire to increase. But we were also advised to be modest, as reflected in the saying that the branch of a tree which is laden with fruit always bends low.

The philosophy that we were taught advocated equality among all human beings. For example, the Sanskrit verse 'vidya-vinaya-sampanne brahmane gavi hastini suni caiva swa-pake ca panditah sama-darsinah' states that an enlightened person does not and should not make any distinction between people of different castes, creeds, genders, or colours. 'Vasudaiva kutumbakam' translates as 'the world is one family'. And the verse 'aatmavat sarbabhuteshu ya pasyati sa panditah' states that one who sees everyone in himself and himself in everyone will be called an enlightened or learned person.

We were taught that by always doing good deeds and for everyone, our minds would be purified. A pure mind, devoid of bad thoughts, is itself a temple. There was also a warning that youth, money, power, and thoughtlessness can take their toll. I was especially touched by one verse in the Manusmriti, an ancient code of conduct for society, which reads: 'Justice is the one friend who continues to follow you even after death, for everything else is lost along with the body when one dies'. Teachings of this nature left an indelible impression on me: they shaped my ethos in life and prepared me to meet the challenges of the life that I have lived in both the East and the West.[2]

My Indoctrination into the Norms of an Ancient Society

The social norms of the society in which I grew up had changed little for thousands of years; indeed, some of them dated back to Vedic times. The *Times Atlas of Ancient Civilizations*[3] states that the Rig Veda was probably composed towards the end of the Indus Valley

2 A brief account of how these values shaped my life is given in my article entitled 'What Is Missing in Nepal', published by American TV news network CNN (https://edition.cnn.com/2015/04/28/opinions/subedi-nepal-earthquake/index.html); and in an interview with the chief editor of the *Journal of East Asia and International Law* entitled 'Judicial Wisdom' and published in its Spring 2011 issue (vol 4, No 1).

3 Chris Scarre (ed), *The Times Atlas of Ancient Civilizations, Part 6: South Asia* (Times Books Limited, London, 1989), p 6. See also Norman Stone et al. (eds), *Harper Collins Atlas of World History* (3rd edition) (Borders Press in association with Harper Collins, London, 1998), p 16.

civilisation – that is, around 1450 BC. At that time, everyday life – from birth to death, and from dawn to dusk – was heavily regulated by the social norms specified in the Vedas, some of which had the status of religious requirements. Most of the norms, especially those relating to hygiene, had been refined over centuries and served society well.

Nature worshipping, which began in antiquity, was still the norm. Upon rising from bed in the morning, a Brahmin's first task of the day was to pray to Mother Earth and seek forgiveness for any harm that might be caused to her and to the environment from human activities during the day ahead. This prayer was followed by a prayer to the sun god to thank him for rising every day to end the darkness and for sustaining life on earth. Next was a prayer for the wellbeing of all creatures in this world and for peace on earth, in the sky, in the waters, in outer space, in all forms of nature (including trees, medicinal herbs, and vegetation), in all gods and deities, and in the universe as a whole.

The lessons learned from all sorts of epidemics, pandemics, plagues, and other mass illnesses and health hazards over the centuries informed rigid rules on personal hygiene and social norms in order to keep people healthy and safe. Taking a shower and changing one's clothes every morning was compulsory. So too was the requirement to change one's clothes and put on a clean white dhoti to enter the dining area, without shoes or slippers, for the two main meals of the day. The hearth, the kitchen, and the whole dining area were regarded as sacred and were cleaned every day both after cooking meals and after serving food.

Strict discipline was maintained to ensure that there was no exploitation of the weaker and vulnerable by the more powerful, even within the family. A strict monogamous marriage was the ideal. At the wedding, the couple would take seven steps together and make the following seven vows:

> Let us take the first step to sharing the responsibility of providing for our household; Let us take the second step to strengthen our mind, body and soul to meet life's needs; Let us take the third step to accomplish wealth and prosperity through righteous means; Let us take the fourth step to acquire happiness through mutual love, respect and trust; Let us take the fifth step to raise strong, virtuous and courageous children; Let us take the sixth step towards spiritual values and longevity; Let us take the seventh step to stay best friends in this lifelong matrimony.

Upon getting married, a man and woman became the rulers of their household, and the woman was called upon to be the queen. Many rules concerned the regulation of sex, and the power dynamics among family members were considered in setting these rules. For instance, a younger sister-in-law was required to cover her head with a dhoti or scarf when appearing before an older brother-in-law and was never meant to touch him. The girls of the family were regarded as sacred until they reached puberty or menstruated for the first time. There were strict rules on self-isolation to be observed for 10 to 12 days after a death in the family. Diseases akin to Ebola, SARS, and COVID-19 would have come and gone in the past, and rules on quarantine and isolation seem to have been introduced in response. Any unnecessary or undesirable physical contact with other people in the family or society was to be avoided – so much so that even greetings were carried out in the form of a 'Namaste' rather than a handshake.

Since we, as Brahmins, were to lead an austere life devoted to learning and imparting knowledge, we were forbidden to eat anything that was deemed to be a stimulant, such as eggs, onions, or garlic. Furthermore, we were not to eat meat or meat products from animals that were viewed as being reared in unhygienic conditions, such as pork and chicken. Only lean and what was believed to be 'clean' meat from animals that roamed in nature was permitted, and venison was preferred. Brahmins were directed to remain celibate until the age of 25. My father used to say that I could marry whoever I liked, once I had completed my university education, had reached the age of 25, and was in a gainful profession or occupation, whether employed or self-employed.

Cattle served as currency since the advent of the agricultural revolution. The practice of giving a cow or a piece of agricultural land to a priest, rather than money, was the norm in Vedic society and still existed centuries later when I was growing up. Cows were regarded as sacred because they were the most useful animal for human survival in antiquity, and they are still considered sacred in much of the Hindu world to this day. Indeed, all living and non-living resources that were vital to the survival of the people were perceived as sacred – cattle as much as rivers, lakes, and mountains, which were thus protected from pollution. The Ganges river was characterised as holy, as millions of people depended on it as their sole water resource. It is not that rivers or cows were worshipped, but their utility was appreciated and the need to preserve them and utilise them sustainably was recognised through these practices.

We were taught that lasting friendships can be forged only among people who are one's equals in wealth, intellect, industry, and education. It was said that a fellow citizen can be counted as a friend after ten years, a fellow artist after five years, a priest who knows the Vedas after three years, and people related by birth after only a short while. Individuals should be subject to the utmost scrutiny before accepting them as friends, and a friendship terminates as soon as the reason for it dies. No one is dear to another unless there is a gain involved. Kindness is the greatest virtue; anger is an all-powerful enemy; and greed is a never-ending disease. It is pointless to argue your case where no distinction is made between good and evil, right and wrong. As the Vedic society was matriarchal, the status of women in society was higher than that of men. It was said that a teacher was more important than 10 instructors, a father was more important than 100 teachers, and a mother was more important than 1,000 fathers.

There were also teachings on the need to enhance one's personal qualities. A man becomes a good person through good work and an evil person through evil deeds. The ability to rule oneself allows one to rule the world. A good man is one whose blood never gets heated by pride. The goddess of prosperity resides in an eloquent person, an active person, and an attentive person. Man is more than what he knows about himself. We were told that some of the key beliefs shared among Hindus were as follows:

- Truth is eternal.
- Brahman is truth and reality.
- The Vedas are the ultimate authority.
- Everyone should strive to achieve dharma.
- Individual souls are immortal.
- The goal of the individual soul is moksha (or salvation).

The two major Hindu festivals, Navaratri and Deepavali, were the highlights of the year. Navaratri was celebrated within the family as well as publicly, and we got new clothes for the celebrations. Navaratri and Deepavali were both held in autumn, right after the monsoon season, when the natural world was flourishing and beautiful flowers, such marigolds, were blossoming in abundance. This was also the time when people would redecorate their houses, both inside and outside, to repair the damage caused by the monsoon rains.

My Arrival in Shangri-La

After passing the SLCE, I left my village and headed for the Nepalese capital, Kathmandu, to join Tribhuvan University – the one and only university in the country. I had intended to do a science degree but had to change my plans because by the time I received the results of the SLCE, it was too late to apply for admission to the science programme. This is because we had to wait for a print copy of the national newspaper, *Gorkhapatra*, to arrive in our village, as our exam results were published in the paper. Back in those days, it was a two-day trek on foot from my village to catch a bus to Kathmandu. Still, I was fortunate in this respect as it had taken my older siblings five days to walk to Kathmandu to obtain their university education. Luckily, since my older siblings' school days, a road had been built to connect Kathmandu and Pokhara, a tourist town that was popular with hippies at the time. I was able to catch a bus to Kathmandu after only a two days walk from my village to the bus route.

It was on my way to Kathmandu that I saw a motor car for the first time in my life and had my first drink of Coca-Cola when I was 15 years old. The sight of a moving motor car amazed me, and evoked both apprehension and excitement in me. This was my first close encounter with modernity. Prior to this, my only contact with modern forms of transport was the occasional aircraft spotted high up in the sky over my village, heading perhaps from Singapore or Malaysia to Europe. In my eyes, those aircraft resembled shooting stars as the rumble of their engines echoed through the hills and mountains.

After the exam results had been published, I travelled to Kathmandu for the first time in my life. There, I was told that I had missed the deadline to apply for a science degree and my only option was to apply for a law degree. After passing the entrance exam, I began to study law at Tribhuvan University. After the successful completion of my first year of study, I won the Jehendar Chhatrabritti, a scholarship awarded to the best student of the year.

During my time in Kathmandu, I felt as though I was living in some kind of Shangri-La: an earthly paradise, an enduringly happy land, isolated from the rest of the world. Located approximately 1,400 metres above sea level in the heart of a bowl-shaped valley, Kathmandu is also known as the city of temples. There are numerous ancient Hindu and Buddhist temples and pagodas dotted across the city, and some sort of religious or local festival takes place more or less every day of the year to worship different gods and goddesses.

The air descending down from the Himalayas was fresh and clean in Kathmandu at that time, and the view of the surrounding mountains was mesmerising. The pace of life was slow, and the people were warm and hospitable. Modern industry and transport had not yet polluted the landscape of the valley. Under both Hinduism and Buddhism – the country's two main religions – people enjoyed personal liberty, including religious freedom. However, they enjoyed only few political rights. Dissent was allowed only up to a point and political parties were banned. The country was ruled by King Birendra as the executive monarch, who was largely a benevolent ruler, but the absence of genuine political rights troubled people like me, and so I became a student leader and activist for political rights.

My Introduction to the Study and Practice of Human Rights

During my first year as a law student, I met party political activists who persuaded me to stand for the position of president of a student organisation known as the Gandaki Students Union. I won the election and became a fervent student human rights activist. I began to write articles and speeches criticising the government's one-party regime, known as the 'party-less panchayat system', as the country was ruled by the king as an absolute monarch. I decided to join a student movement aimed at overthrowing this system of government and changing the nature of the monarchy to a constitutional institution. Consequently, I was arrested and sent to Bhadragol Jail (meaning 'messy prison', which it was in both practical and logistical terms). I faced a harsh punishment for my political convictions in favour of democracy, human rights, and the rule of law.

I was arrested at dawn at my home in Thamel, a hippy enclave in Kathmandu, and was taken into police custody, where I was kept incommunicado for two weeks for interrogation. It was the hot month of May, and life was unbearable in the small, stuffy cell in which I was held without adequate food or water – conditions which most likely caused the damage to one of my kidneys. I learned much later in life that one of my kidneys has long been defunct and I must have incurred this harm during my detention.

After two weeks in the small police cell, I was transferred to the central prison, where I was held as a political prisoner and treated more humanely. I was allowed to interact with other political prisoners, to read books, and to exercise in the open air. Although I was relieved about these changes, I was not told what the charges against me were until the third week of my imprisonment, when I was handed a notice stating that the administration had deemed it necessary to detain me in order to prevent me from committing acts against law and order – meaning against the autocratic political system. However, the notice said nothing about the length of my detention in prison and whether I would be presented before a judicial authority and tried for alleged offences of a political nature. That uncertainty troubled me a lot and my future looked bleak at the time, as many political prisoners often were imprisoned for months – and sometimes years – without trial under this law.

While I was imprisoned, my fellow students held daily demonstrations demanding my release and the release of all student leaders who had been arrested and imprisoned along with me for participating in the pro-democracy movement. What sustained me in prison was my belief that the Eton-educated king of Nepal would allow the Nepalese people to decide on their preferred system of governance and enjoy their political rights. I also had faith in the role of the modern international human rights agenda and in the power of the people to modernise Nepal's culturally conservative but highly politically conscious society. The king eventually bowed to public pressure and decided to hold a referendum to determine the future political system of the country, and I was released from prison. Enjoying my freedom, I campaigned vigorously for a multi-party system of government in the run-up to the referendum. However, when the results of the referendum were declared to be in favour of the existing party-less panchayat system and the leader of the main opposition party, BP Koirala, accepted the outcome of the referendum, I decided to quit active politics and pursue a professional legal career instead.

Incidentally, my experience of imprisonment in Kathmandu in 1980 inspired me to write my book entitled *Human Rights in Eastern Civilisations* (published by Edward Elgar Publishing, a British academic publishing house), as well as this memoir, during the national Covid-19 lockdowns in the UK in 2020/21.

After completing my law degree, which was delayed for a year because of the referendum, I was called to the Bar in Nepal in 1981. A year later, I decided to join the government service and sat the Public Service Commission Examination for law officers. Having passed the examination, I was initially appointed as a district public prosecutor within the Office of the Attorney-General and was then deputised to the Royal Commission on Judicial Reform. While working for the commission during the day, I spent evenings and weekends writing my first book, on the subject of Nepalese administrative law. The publication of this book by a reputable publisher brought in the additional revenue needed to supplement my governmental salary. Upon completion of the commission's work, I was posted to the International Law and Treaties Division of the Ministry of Law and Justice, where my job involved writing periodic country reports to various UN human rights treaty bodies, among other things. This task provided me with the opportunity to hone my skills in researching and writing on human rights matters.

Family Achievements and Tragedies

On 10 December 1984 – Human Rights Day – I married Kokila, a girl from eastern Nepal who was studying for her MA at the same university in Kathmandu where I was studying for my masters. We were married according to Hindu tradition in Dharan, Nepal. I was the first of the Subedi clan – a traditional family from western Nepal – to marry a woman of his choice from a faraway part of the country and from a family completely unknown to my family. This was regarded as progressive at the time in Nepal.

The first major tragedy that struck us in our newly married life was the loss of our first child, a baby daughter, in September 1985. Unfortunately, while pregnant, Kokila caught jaundice. At the time, jaundice during pregnancy was a very serious condition, which often caused the death of the unborn child and jeopardised the life of the mother. Kokila had to be admitted to a communicable disease hospital in Kathmandu, where our child was born prematurely; she was then kept in an incubation cubicle in a different hospital. During our daughter's short life, I travelled a few times a day to the teaching hospital in Maharajganj, situated at one end of the Kathmandu valley to the north, to be with our newborn daughter, and then to the communicable disease hospital in Teku, at the other end of town to the south, to be with my wife, who was seriously ill. This was a very challenging time for us all and a real test of my own resilience.

Despite all attempts to save her life, our baby daughter died when she was just nine days old. I was heartbroken and distraught. I could not summon the courage to tell my wife, so a close relation of ours stepped in to do so. We both were grief-stricken to the core and have not fully recovered from the tragedy to this day; grief is a never-ending journey, and we are still grieving. Kokila's own life was also in danger due to the jaundice and some of my relations feared that she would not survive the illness. After losing our daughter, I stayed by my wife's bedside in hospital to support her, hoping and praying for her recovery. Fortunately, Kokila eventually regained her health; she is a strong woman and her fighting spirits are high.

It was while working in the International Law Division of the Ministry of Law and Justice in Nepal that I was awarded a British Council scholarship (today called a Chevening scholarship) to study for a master's degree in law at a university in England. The opportunity to study law at postgraduate level in England was exciting, and Kokila and I prepared for our move overseas. To say goodbye to Kokila's family, who lived in the small village of Dharan, we boarded an overnight bus from Kathmandu. Tragically, halfway through the journey, the night bus came off the road, rolled down a hill, and crashed on the bank of a river that was swollen due to the heavy monsoon rain, close to the village of Mugleni, between Kathmandu and the tourist city of Pokhara.

Eight passengers, including the bus driver, lost their lives on that fateful night on Friday 13 June 1986. Kokila and I both survived, but with massive injuries. Kokila had been knocked unconscious, and we were transported in an ambulance to the country's main hospital in Kathmandu. I was discharged after two days of treatment and my wife after five days. There was barely a fortnight left for me to recover from the accident and leave for Britain for my studies. Ever since this accident, I have tried to avoid travelling on Friday 13 of any month.

Thankfully, Kokila's mother came from Dharan to Kathmandu to support her, and both Kokila and her mother advised me not to miss this once-in-a-lifetime opportunity to pursue my postgraduate studies in the UK. With a heavy heart, and still reeling from the aftermath of the tragedies that had befallen us in quick succession – Kokila's illness, the loss of our first child, and the major bus accident – I left Nepal for the UK. We had agreed that once I had settled into my studies, Kokila would join me in the UK.

The move to the UK was a major turning point in my life. I embarked on this journey to a completely unknown country still recovering from my injuries sustained in the bus accident. I had a British Airways flight ticket, issued by the British Council office in Kathmandu, for London via New Delhi. I set foot on British soil for the first time on 26 June 1986. London was glittering in the summer sun, and the city was celebrating the football World Cup like a festival. Upon my arrival at Gatwick, I was greeted by a representative of the British Council, Miss Jedda Helliwell, and taken to my hotel in Piccadilly Circus, where I watched television for the first time in my life (television was not yet available in Nepal). I stayed in London for three or four days to explore the city before heading north to the University of Hull to commence my LLM in international law.

After the bus accident, I recognised the preciousness of life even more acutely and felt driven to make a valuable contribution to society. When I commenced my studies at the University of Hull, I decided to specialise in international human rights law and rekindle my passion for human rights. The flashback to my time as a human rights activist and the weeks I had spent in jail for fighting for good causes also served as an inspiration to specialise in human rights law. As law is a discipline in the service of others, I thought that a law degree would better equip me to assist those fighting for democracy, human rights, and the rule of law.

To my surprise and delight, I completed my LLM at the University of Hull with distinction and was awarded a prize for best student of the year. This instilled me with greater confidence and drove my ambitions to contribute to wider society. The education that I received at Hull prepared me well to venture out into the world and develop myself as an international law scholar. Our class resembled a mini-UN, as my fellow students hailed from all across the world. Through the influence of luminaries such as William Wilberforce, who led the campaign to abolish slavery in the UK, Hull had come to be seen as closely connected to the causes of human rights, liberty, and emancipation. The city was buzzing at the time with lively debates on contemporary global issues taking place frequently.

A Royal Appointment

After graduating from the University of Hull, I applied to the University of Oxford for admission to its doctoral programme in law, before returning to Nepal. The relationship between Nepal and India was becoming increasingly strained at the time, and negotiations on the renewal of trade and transit treaties between the two countries were going nowhere. The situation soon escalated when India effectively imposed a sort of economic blockade on landlocked Nepal. Fatefully, I had undertaken a research project at Hull on the trade and transit rights of landlocked countries during my studies. Now back in Nepal, I published my research findings in the main national daily English newspaper, *The Rising Nepal*, outlining Nepal's rights as a landlocked country in international law. King Birendra learned of my newspaper articles and asked his palace secretaries to find out who I was and where I was working. I was then contacted by the palace secretaries, who informed me that the king was willing to receive me in audience.

When I went to see the king, he told me that he had found my articles informative and useful, adding that they clearly articulated Nepal's position in international law. The king consequently asked me to work as his adviser on international legal matters. I thus became a member of the Ministry of Foreign Affairs taskforce on all aspects of Indo-Nepal relations, constituted under the chairmanship of the then foreign minister, Shailendra Kumar Upadhayaya. The king instructed the diplomatic services to send a copy of my newspaper articles published in *The Rising Nepal*, together with a *note verbale*, to all foreign diplomatic missions in Nepal and all Nepalese embassies abroad, and to the UN, in order to convey Nepal's position to the international community.

In summer 1989, the Ninth Non-Aligned Summit Conference was held in Belgrade. The king had planned a meeting on the sidelines of the summit with the then prime minister of India, Rajiv Gandhi, on bilateral matters, including the blockade. Impressed by my work as a member of the taskforce for Indo-Nepal relations, the king asked me to join the Nepalese delegation headed up by him, so that I could advise him on international legal matters during his dialogue with Gandhi. Unfortunately, however, this dialogue between the Indian prime minister and the Nepalese king in Belgrade did not resolve the differences between the two countries.

I returned from Belgrade to Kathmandu, where I eagerly awaited the outcome of my application to the University of Oxford. Since the postal system was unreliable in Nepal, I worried that the letter might not reach me in time. So I made the following pact with the local postman: I promised him 10 rupees for every letter delivered on time and 20 rupees for international mail. One fine morning, the postman rushed towards me waving a letter from the University of Oxford; I paid him 50 rupees that day. The letter confirmed that I had been offered admission to the doctoral programme in law at the University of Oxford, as well as a British Foreign and Commonwealth Office (FCO) scholarship.

While I was overjoyed at the news, I now faced a professional and personal dilemma. I was working as a legal adviser to King Birendra and the country was in crisis. Should I stay in the country to support the king as best I could? Would my doctoral studies better equip me to advise the king in the future? I decided to inform the king of the offer for PhD study at Oxford and seek his permission to take it up. I went to see him in the Narayanhiti Royal Palace. Upon telling him the news, he pondered for a minute, and then said:

> Although I cannot afford to lose you at this point in time in the country, you have been offered a once-in-a-lifetime opportunity and I do not wish you to lose it. You would be the first Nepali to carry out doctoral research study at Oxford. It is a matter pride for Nepal too. Therefore, you should go; but you should remain in touch with me and continue to advise me from Oxford on issues of national importance.

These were the words of a big-hearted, gentlemanly monarch who deeply valued education; he himself had been to Eton and he recognised the advantages of having an advisor who has earned his degree at Oxford, an academic institution of outstanding merit. When I told my wife about the conversation, she observed that the king had become something akin to a father figure to me.

The second challenge was family related. My wife was six months pregnant at the time and we were having a house built in Kathmandu to start a new life there. My professional life was also on a very good trajectory: I had become an adviser to the king at the young age of 31 and there was much in store for me in Nepal. However, when my wife and I weighed up all the options and the pros and cons of each one, we decided that we would go to Oxford together. I did not wish to leave my heavily pregnant wife behind in Nepal, especially in view of the complications of the first pregnancy and the loss of our first child three years earlier. So we left Kathmandu together on 30 September 1989, as my programme of doctoral study at the University of Oxford was to commence the following week.

Bringing Pride to King and Country

While in Oxford, I continued to advise King Birendra on international legal matters, and carried on doing so long after I had completed my doctoral studies and had embarked on an academic career in the UK. I was the first Nepali to obtain a DPhil from Oxford and in addition, I received a prestigious prize for outstanding DPhil thesis of the year. Upon hearing the news, the king sent me a letter of congratulations in which he expressed his pride in my academic achievements. The whole nation seemed to echo the king's sentiment when the Nepalese media published the news of the first Nepali earning a doctorate at Oxford. After completing my DPhil, I began my academic career in the UK and kept on advising the king throughout the 1990s on many constitutional and international legal issues. I also met the king in London each time he visited for a medical check-up. He was always thinking about the country, asking me to explore the viability of new ideas to make Nepal more prosperous and to report back to him accordingly.

The king was committed to democratic norms and a constitutional monarchy. He ruled the country largely as a benevolent monarch – especially after the referendum held in 1980, in which he gave the people the power to decide what form of government they wanted for the country. He went one step further in 1990 when he agreed to switch from an executive monarchy to a constitutional monarchy. It was a pleasure and an honour to work for such a gentlemanly and enlightened monarch of this Himalayan kingdom with a rich heritage and an ancient civilisation. In recognition of my services to the nation, King Birendra awarded me a high-level state honour – the Suprabal Gokhadaxinbahu – in 1998 and I returned to Nepal to attend the investiture at the royal palace. The king smiled brightly when he decorated me and thanked me for my work. It was a memorable day and a proud moment in my life.

I was devastated when the king was killed in a palace shootout in June 2001. The world had lost a model monarch of the twentieth century. All of the major international news networks, including the BBC and CNN, reported live the tragic events at the royal palace in Kathmandu. It was another very sad time in my life and I struggled to sleep for many nights. It so happened that, at the time, I was organising an international conference in London on international watercourses law, with special reference to the sharing and management of the water resources of the Ganges between the three riparian states, Bangladesh, India, and Nepal. The conference was held the day after the king's assassination. At the start of the conference, I read out a message of condolence, and all of the participants who had assembled from all over the world joined me in paying homage to this eminent Nepalese monarch. We also passed a resolution to acknowledge the king's contributions to promoting peace at home and abroad through his pioneering idea of a zone of peace (ZOP) and his commitment to democracy and the establishment of a constitutional monarchy in Nepal. This was one way of coping with the shocking news from Nepal and mourning the king's death.

2 The Oxford Years and the Triple Gain

Inspired by the City of Spires

Upon arriving at Oxford from Nepal with my pregnant wife in October 1989 to commence my doctoral research, I was asked to enrol on the DPhil programme initially as an MLitt student. In the third term, I would be required to complete a transfer of status from MLitt to full DPhil student. Thus, significant demands were placed on me from the outset, and I was keen to settle my family into our accommodation as quickly as possible so that I could focus on my research and writing. While the holders of Commonwealth scholarships – students from former British colonies – benefited from a family allowance, I, as someone from a country that had never been colonised, had only a single scholarship, and hence money remained tight throughout my years at Oxford. Unlike many of my fellow DPhil students, I had neither the time, the money, nor the inclination to attend freshers' week for undergraduates or introduction week for us mature students, or to visit the pubs in Oxford. Rather, I relied heavily on a second-hand shop in north Oxford run by research students for research students where I bought many of our household items.

The academic environment at Oxford was superb. The professors were very supportive and encouraging and the university attracted the great and good from the world of international law to deliver guest lectures. My main DPhil supervisor, Professor Christine Gray, gave me enough independence to develop my ideas while carefully and thoroughly scrutinising what I produced and offering constructive comments. I was fortunate to have a person of such formidable intellect as my supervisor.

Professor Ian Brownlie, the Chichele Professor of Public International Law at Oxford, was also exceptionally kind to me; as was Professor Sir Adam Roberts, the Montague Burton Professor of International Relations. Both received richly deserved knighthoods

DOI: 10.4324/9781003271543-2

later in their careers. They often jointly chaired the Trinity Term seminars on 'The Role of Law in the International Community', which were the highlight of our academic calendar. There is a thin line between international law and international relations, so it was a uniquely enlightening experience for us to hear these two luminaries discuss how international law operated in the contemporary international community. Each professor was in a league of his own and second to none in his field in his time.

For reasons best known to themselves, both had a certain affinity for me. Years later, when I was working in The Hague, I would have lunch or dinner with them whenever they visited the city to deliver lectures either at The Hague Academy of International Law or the Asser Institute, or at Clingendael – the Netherlands Institute of International Relations. During one of his visits to The Hague, Professor Roberts invited me back to Oxford to deliver a lecture in the seminar series that he chaired. He also entertained me at his home in the evening and I was touched by his generosity. When I later started to visit the University of Oxford from Leeds to teach on the master's programme in international human rights law, Professor Roberts and I met up several times. On each occasion, our conversation was a source of great inspiration and encouragement.

Professor Brownlie was equally an impressive intellectual and a charming, curious conversation partner. My PhD viva was held in his splendid study at All Souls College in July 1993 and whenever I subsequently returned to Oxford, he invited me to lunch at the college. Once he gave me a tour of his private apartments at All Souls to show me an excellent collection of maps of the Himalayan region and other historical documents and publications on South Asia that he had collated over the years. He also continued to support me in my endeavours. When I became professor of international law and director of the newly established Centre for International Governance at the University of Leeds, I invited him to inaugurate the centre and deliver the first lecture, and he kindly accepted my invitation and visited Leeds with his wife, Christine.

Had he lived to see me become a QC in the UK and receive the Oxford Doctor of Civil Law (DCL), the pinnacle of the career of a lawyer and a law academic, Professor Brownlie would have been proud of me – as my father and King Birendra would have been. Tragically, however, Professor Brownlie was killed in 2010 in a car accident while on a family holiday in Cairo. Christine survived the accident with injuries, and I visited her as soon as she had recovered to pass on my condolences. As I was about to leave, she said: 'Surya, Ian used to like you. Therefore, if you wish, please feel free to take any books from his collection'. I accepted the offer gratefully and selected a few books – among them, four volumes of the series entitled *The Historical Records of the Survey of India* by the surveyor generals of India, including George Everest, after whom Mount Everest is named. I brought them home and kept them safe; at the time, I did not realise how significant they would become to my work for Nepal a decade later.

When the issue of boundary encroachment by India became a crucial political topic in 2020, the Nepalese government established an expert group to collect evidence and develop a strategy for boundary negotiations with India, and appointed me as a member. We soon realised that we needed authentic maps published by British India showing the disputed territory within the national boundaries of Nepal after the war with the British in 1814–15 and the conclusion of the Treaty of Sugauli, a peace treaty which had stated that Nepal's western border would be the River Kalee. I studied all kinds of historical records, articles, and maps – one of which was Volume III of *The Historical Records of the Survey of India*. To my delight, this volume from the home of Professor Brownlie included the most authentic maps and descriptions of the boundary between British India and Nepal published by the Government of India. All four volumes will remain with me for the rest of my life as permanent reminders of my professor and friend.

Adjusting to a New Life in Oxford

The move to Oxford from Nepal necessitated a period of adjustment as we acclimatised to life in this new environment and our family expanded. Upon our arrival, I was invited to attend the matriculation at my college and was given a strict dress code for the ceremony, college dinners, and examinations. The dress code listed something called 'sub-fusc', which included a gown and a dinner jacket, among other items. I was based at Exeter, a Turl Street college, located in the centre of Oxford next to the main Bodleian Library, so the obvious places to source the required items of clothing were the shops in Turl Street, which were very upmarket. I vividly remember paying a hefty £35 for a cotton shirt to go with my sub-fusc; it was expensive by the standards of 1993 and even more so for a student from Nepal.

Had I enquired about what I would need in Oxford before arriving, I could have bought similar shirts for a fraction of the price in Nepal and brought them with me; or had the ceremony not taken place so soon after my arrival, I could have acquired them in Oxford's budget stores. This expensive lesson taught us that we needed to get streetwise fast.

Three months after our arrival in Oxford, as I worked tirelessly to prepare for the MLitt examination, our son Pranay was born on 6 January 1990, on a bright but wintry afternoon. The following summer was reportedly the hottest on record, and we thoroughly enjoyed our first English summer with our baby son, visiting the parks and gardens of Oxford and the surrounding areas, including Blenheim Palace in Woodstock.

Meanwhile, my DPhil studies were progressing well and Kokila and I decided to have a second baby, so that our children could grow up together. In May 1991, Kokila fell pregnant and – with the help of a doctor friend of mine, and without Kokila's knowledge, as she did not want to know yet – I found out that we were expecting a girl. I was filled with joy. During the Christmas sales that year, I bought plenty of baby clothes for a girl and hid them from Kokila in my cupboard at Exeter College. Our daughter Anita was born on the night of a beautiful full moon on 19 February 1992 – Democracy Day in Nepal.

However, there were financial challenges to contend with, as my single scholarship did not pay enough to support and sustain a family of four. Therefore, Kokila secured a part-time position at a local private tutorial company, leaving home very early in the mornings to work for two to three hours and returning in time for me to get to university by 9:00 am. We also applied for an allotment – a plot of agricultural land managed by the local council – in north Oxford to grow vegetables and we worked on the allotment during the weekends. This yielded an additional benefit, as our allotment neighbours often gave us lots of their surplus produce.

As our financial situation became more precarious due to the costs of raising two young children, Prime Minister Thatcher's privatisation programme came to our rescue. British public utility companies were being privatised one after another. I soon realised that people were making money within a matter of months – or even weeks – by buying shares when a company was being privatised and then selling them when the company was floated on the stock market. As residents of the United Kingdom we were entitled to buy shares in these companies, but we did not have the money to invest; so I asked my bank for an overdraft.

The bank manager agreed to lend us some money, warning us that share prices can go down as well as up. I was prepared to take the risk and bought the shares, nonetheless. To our delight, the price of those shares rose when the companies were floated on the stock market; we sold the shares quickly and returned the money we owed to the bank, keeping the profit. We earned some extra money – albeit small amounts – from repeating this process once or twice. The additional income helped to sustain us financially at Oxford; so I owe thanks to the then prime minister, Mrs Thatcher, for the opportunities that her privatisation programme afforded us.

The Development, Award, and Publication of My DPhil

My Oxford DPhil research project focused on analysing and developing the concept of a ZOP in international law. Since the escalation of the arms race during the Cold War, the world had become increasingly unsafe. The member states of the Warsaw Pact and NATO sought to utilise the global commons for military purposes and to attract smaller and weaker non-aligned countries to join their cause. Consequently, there was momentum in the 1960s, 1970s, and 1980s to designate both land and maritime areas in different parts of the world as ZOPs, nuclear-weapons-free zones, or nuclear-free zones. Several initiatives had been undertaken both within and outside the UN to establish ZOPs in various parts of the globe.

In my research, I examined state practice on maritime ZOPs and whether the concept of ZOPs was consistent with existing principles of international law – especially the freedom of the seas – and whether the state practice on ZOPs had solidified into a rule of customary international law. This was followed by an examination of the proposals for land ZOPs. My study then assessed the extent to which the principles that underpin traditional concepts such as neutrality and demilitarised zones, as well as similar emerging principles, could be applied to the concept of the ZOP.

The night before my viva was agonising. I was unable to fall asleep until about 3:00 am and woke up at 6:00 am. I had started preparing for my viva weeks before, honing my thoughts on the legal arguments that I had advanced in my thesis by reading more around the issues.

The day before the viva, I read my entire thesis of 300 pages and in the process spotted four minor typographical errors, which mortified me. I feared I might fail the examination due to these typographical errors.

Luckily, on the following day, I thoroughly enjoyed the viva and there was no mention of the typographical errors in the thesis. My examiners – one from Oxford and one from Cambridge – were the most accomplished experts in the field. During the viva, the external examiner from Cambridge noted that in my thesis I had disagreed with him on a point of law. I worried that he might fail me due to this difference of opinion. But, noticing that I was getting nervous about this, he quickly reassured me that although I had disagreed with him on a particular point, my line of argument was plausible and I had presented enough evidence to support my thesis. After the viva, the examiners complimented me on the originality and craftsmanship of my thesis and the rigour of my analysis. I was overwhelmed with joy.

I was also surprised and delighted to be awarded the Dasturzada Pavry Memorial Prize for outstanding doctoral thesis of the year in 1993. I felt that this was a great achievement for someone from a simple village in Nepal and I took real satisfaction from the award. Although I had obtained an LLM with distinction from the University of Hull, it was during my extensive research in this area of law at Oxford that I became a truly confident scholar of international law. Given my responsibilities both as a young student-father of two and as the first Nepali doctoral student at Oxford, I was eager to succeed – and the award of both my DPhil and the prize served as confirmation that I had done so.

Perhaps the crowning glory that wrapped up my time as a student at Oxford was the acceptance of my doctoral thesis for publication by Oxford University Press (OUP) in 1994. Professor Brownlie had advised me to convert my thesis into a book and submit it to OUP, as it offered new and original insights in the field. The reports of OUP's anonymous external referees were both encouraging and helpful. I had already published two law books in Nepal prior to arriving in the UK, but the publication of *Land and Maritime Zones of Peace in International Law* by OUP was a key milestone in my academic career.

I was just as delighted when the book was awarded the annual prize of the British Society of Legal Scholars – formerly known as the Society of Public Teachers of Law in 1997. Receiving an accolade from such an esteemed body of British academics was a source of immense pride and satisfaction. I was touched by the letter from the then president of the Society, Professor Hugh Beal, in which he outlined the views of the assessment panel in deciding to award the prize to me.

Nearly 20 years after graduating from Oxford with a DPhil and experiencing life in The Hague, Hull, London, Leeds, New York, and Washington DC – as either a full professor or a visiting professor – I was invited back to Oxford in 2016 to teach as a visiting faculty member on its master's programme in international human rights law. I was delighted to be back at my alma mater and taught on the programme for five years, until 2021. Returning to Oxford reminded me of my own time at the university, and I enjoyed engaging with the high-calibre students that the programme attracts from all around the world.

Accolades from Oxford

Higher doctorates are earned awards of the University of Oxford that aim to recognise excellence in academic scholarship. The Oxford DCL – the university's highest accolade – is rarely awarded, and only in exceptional cases. In evaluating a DCL application, the judges are asked to consider whether the evidence submitted by the candidate demonstrates excellence in academic scholarship and is:

- Of the absolute highest quality.
- Substantial in scale and in the contribution it has made to knowledge.
- Sustained over time and showing current and continued contributions to scholarship.
- Authoritative and impactful on the work of others.
- Of global reach and international importance within the field.
- Of such breadth or covering such branches of knowledge as are appropriate to the field and in line with disciplinary norms and expectations.

This is a very high threshold to meet. However, after publishing ten books and nearly 60 scholarly articles covering a wide range of areas of international law, I felt confident enough to apply for the DCL in 2018. Almost one year after submission of my application, the University of Oxford informed me that I would be awarded the DCL in recognition of my 'exceptionally insightful and distinctive publications that contain significant and original contributions to the study of law'.

The judges praised me as 'a scholar of uncommon breadth of knowledge and depth of thinking', adding:

> His work is substantial in scale. He is a legal philosopher whose work has had an undoubted impact on the theory of international law, whilst his knowledge of specialist areas of law has permitted him to make specific suggestions for reform. Professor Subedi's academic achievements, combined with his substantial body of publications and engagement with governmental and intergovernmental organizations, demonstrate work of the highest quality sustained over time.

The judges also commented on many of my publications. For example, their feedback on my book entitled *The Effectiveness of the UN Human Rights System* (Routledge 2017) read as follows:

> The book creates a modern vision of the United Nations that could function better in a multipolar world to help secure a better mode of living for more people around the world. Only someone who combines a deep understanding of the U.N. system and of international human rights law with an idealistic yet pragmatic vision of what international organizations can accomplish could have produced this masterful work.

About my article 'The Universality of Human Rights and the UN Human Rights Agenda: The Impact of the Shift of Power to the East and the Resurgence of the BRICs' (*Indian Journal of International Law*, 2015), the judges said:

> [It] shows remarkable breadth of understanding of cultures across Asia, and a sensitive and nuanced analysis of them. His assessment that human rights will not be impeded by the rise of the BRICs and other non-western-centric power polarities is backed by a thoughtful exploration of religious, cultural, and other principles that contribute to the complex mosaic of international human rights law.

They also praised my article titled 'The Concept in Hinduism of "Just War"' (*Journal of Conflict & Security Law*, 2003) for mixing

> philosophy with historical practice to distinguish between righteous and unrighteous wars. The article covers religious texts, the sources of Hindu law, and the contribution of Hinduism to current ideas about

> the laws of war and peace, as well as ideas about where Hinduism could improve the current international approach to the law of war. It is a fascinating and erudite assessment of the role that morality can and should play in the creation of law.

My book entitled *International Investment Law: Reconciling Policy and Principle* (3rd edition, Hart, 2016) elicited the following feedback from the judges:

> Professor Subedi was one of the first scholars to analyse the tension that exists between protecting the interests of investors and the obligations of states to address other core policy concerns, many of which themselves are the subject of obligations in international law, such as international human rights and environmental law. And also one of the first to note the resurgence in support for the Calvo doctrine, which asserts that jurisdiction over investor disputes should be located where the investment is made.

Overall, the judges emphasised the exceptionally broad spectrum that my work covers – 'from areas in international law, ranging across international legal theory, the law of watercourses, international trade law, international investment law, international human rights law, and the law and practice of international organizations' – and acknowledged that '[d]eveloping expertise in any one of these fields can easily be the work of a lifetime'. They concluded that my 'clear expertise in all of these fields more than satisfies any expectations in the legal academic field concerning expected breadth of knowledge', as well as excellence in academic scholarship of the very highest quality.

I felt honoured to receive such outstanding recognition of my work. In reaching their decision, the judges on the panel had comprehensively reviewed many of my publications. They not only commented on the quality of those publications, but also highlighted the global impact of my work. This prestigious award was a matter of great pride for me and my family, as well as for the University of Leeds, where I am now professor of international law. Commenting on the award, Sir Alan Langlands – at the time vice chancellor of the University of Leeds – said:

> I congratulate Professor Subedi on being awarded a Doctor of Civil Law from the University of Oxford. This is appropriate recognition of a broad canon of work on the theory and practice of international law and its impact on human rights and other areas of understanding and policy.

Furthermore, I felt proud when two new prizes were established in my name at the University of Oxford in 2020, in order to recognise outstanding performances by law students – one in human rights law and another for best DPhil thesis of the year in law. The annual Dr Surya Subedi Prize in Human Rights Law is awarded to the undergraduate student who achieves the highest mark in the paper on human rights law in the Final Honour School of Jurisprudence each year. The annual Dr Surya Subedi Prize for the DPhil in Law is awarded to the best doctoral thesis in the Faculty of Law – that is, to the thesis that makes the most exciting, original contribution to the relevant field of scholarship and is best crafted in terms of organisation, style, and presentation. All doctoral students in the Faculty of Law, including criminology and socio-legal studies, are eligible for these awards.

The winner of the first Dr Surya Subedi Prize was announced in December 2021. The Dean of the Oxford Law Faculty stated that 'As one of the largest PhD programmes in the world, we were faced with an embarrassment of riches in selecting a prize winner', before revealing that Dr Ndjodi Ndeunyema had won for his thesis 'Interpreting Water: The Human Right to Water under the Namibian Constitution', which has since been published as a book by the Pretoria University Law Press.

I was touched by Dr Ndjodi Ndeunyema message to me saying that 'the Prize has induced a mini-avalanche of pride and inspiration in Namibia, from where I hail, with the extensive media exposure it has received … The beauty of coming from a small population wise is that such news spreads superfast and the entire country takes pride in such a moment on the "world" stage. It is not helped that one of the local radio's reported that I was the best student at Oxford, according to my octogenarian grandmother. The mainstream papers have given the Subedi Prize accurate reporting however'. The members of the Prize Committee also expressed their gratitude for the prize as it allowed them to laud and spotlight Dr Ndjodi Ndeunyema's 'wonderful project'.

'Look what you have given this bright, promising young man', Maureen A. O'Neill, Director of Development in the Oxford Faculty of Law, writes in an email to me, 'he now has national recognition as an academic. Forgive me for saying I am very proud of you! Thank you, thank you for seeing the possibilities that your prize has offered'. She continues to say that this prize is a celebration of educational excellence and of the understanding that the dissertations of the future will provide valuable insights beyond Oxford Law. I was moved by the enthusiasm tangible in all the messages, and by the pride and joy that emanate from Dr Ndjodi Ndeunyema's lines as he describes the impact of the award on himself and his immediate environment.

The Oxford Influence

During my years of research at Oxford, the world was going through a tumultuous period, which was exciting for us students of international law and international relations. The Berlin Wall came down; Communism collapsed in Europe; the Soviet Union disintegrated; the Cold War came to an end; and the first Gulf War took place. Each of these international events made our studies even more relevant, and the university attracted influential speakers on the subjects of the day from all over the world. I was a college representative in the Oxford branch of Amnesty International and campaigned actively on human rights-related issues around the globe, including writing letters to dictators in far-flung states asking them to release human rights defenders from prisons in their countries. Due to my deep-rooted respect for human rights defenders, and my experience of working with human rights defenders in both Nepal and Cambodia, I have dedicated this memoir to them.

I also joined the Oxford Union debating society as a life member and benefited significantly from its activities – although I am unsure whether my life membership is still valid today. I attended talks and group discussions run by the Quaker Society of Oxford in St Giles, which similarly attracted top speakers from British politics, including Labour leader Tony Benn and Liberal-Democrat leader Shirley Williams, both of whom inspired me with their formidable oratory. A further source of inspiration was Chris Patten, a model political intellectual, who, at the time of writing this memoir, is serving as the Chancellor of the University of Oxford. He is a liberal Tory and an 'up to a point' man – a phrase that he uses frequently in his writings, including his seminal book *East and West*.

Looking back, my Oxford years were pivotal to my academic education and development: I broadened my horizons; developed myself as a global citizen; became part of several networks of intellectuals from around the globe; and obtained my DPhil. I could do so in large part thanks to the unstinting efforts of my wife, Kokila, who worked hard to keep the family together while I spent much of my time in the Bodleian Library. I also recall with gratitude the wonderful welcome and generous support given to my wife and me by Sir Richard Norman, the then rector of Exeter College; and by the college bursar, who provided woollen blankets made in Witney and other household items to help us, a young Nepalese family who had just arrived in Oxford, to survive the cold winter.

Oxford has also shaped the lives of my son and daughter in different ways. Although maintaining a family of four on a single scholarship meant that our financial situation was challenging, we enjoyed our years in the city. We lived in Summertown House – a university accommodation that was reserved for research students with families. From the age of two, Pranay went to the crèche at the University of Oxford, which provided a solid foundation for his education. The fees were not particularly high for the going rate at the time, but they were high for us. However, when we received his first certificate from the nursery with 'University of Oxford' marked on the letterhead, we were pleased with our investment in his early education. The report said that he had 'an enviable command of English in someone so young' and was 'a very able child' and concluded: 'He is well established in his educational life'. Indeed, Pranay went on to do very well in his education, obtaining a very good first degree from Warwick University and an MBA from the Chicago Booth Business School. He has now settled in the US, working for a private equity firm.

Anita excelled in her education at a large grammar school in North London and eventually became head girl, before returning to the place of her birth to read law. I have returned to my alma mater for many reasons over the years, and one of them was to bring Anita back to Oxford at the start of each new term of her law degree. I had studied at Exeter College and she was studying next door at Lincoln College – another Turl Street college right behind the main Bodleian Library. On one of my visits to Oxford to see Anita, we compared our lives as students at Oxford, 22 years apart. We were thrilled to discover that her human rights law tutor, Professor Sandra Freedman, was also my tutor at Exeter over two decades earlier. Having studied law at Oxford, Anita also qualified as an associate member of an informal dining club in London set up by Dr James Busuttil, Dr Chaloka Beyani, Dr Phoebe Okowa, Dr Chris Staker, and myself, after we had all completed our DPhils in law together at Oxford.

While Oxford has left a permanent mark on my life, and the lives of my family, I believe that I have also left a permanent mark on Oxford, in the form of the two annual prizes established in my name after I was awarded the DCL in 2019. This has been a source of immense pride and satisfaction for me – a man from a simple village in Nepal.

When we eventually left the City of Spires after I had completed my DPhil, a friend observed that my Oxford years had been 'productive', both intellectually and personally: 'You are leaving with a DPhil in law, with a prize for the best thesis of the year, and with two children – a triple gain!' I agreed wholeheartedly.

3 Life as a Global Citizen in Global Britain

Starting Out in Academia

My Oxford years were transformative for me in so many ways. During the three years of intensively researching and writing my doctoral thesis, I developed a passion for further research that would extend the frontiers of knowledge in international law in general, and international human rights law and the law of peace in particular. In the Upanishads, it is said that knowledge is a means to freedom; and it is this freedom that I wanted both to foster for myself and to exercise by contributing to my chosen academic fields. My DPhil was a passport to an independent life for me. I no longer wished to have a regular occupation in the government service in Nepal or elsewhere; I wanted the freedom to fulfil my aspirations as a scholar and British academia offered marvellous opportunities to do so.

Receiving the prize for outstanding DPhil thesis of the year encouraged me to convert my thesis into a book rather than allowing it to gather dust in the archives of the Bodleian Library. I also consulted my DPhil supervisor, Professor Christine Gray, to discuss the possibility of pursuing a career in British academia. Although I had taught international law to undergraduate students in the final year of my DPhil, I was not confident in my ability to deliver lectures on a variety of subjects and to large student groups. Professor Gray reassured me, saying:

> You have taught international law to undergraduates here at Oxford and student feedback has been positive. If you can teach one law subject, you can teach any other law subject, provided you are given adequate time to prepare for it. I am confident that you will succeed in British academia.

DOI: 10.4324/9781003271543-3

With these words of encouragement in mind, I scanned the academic job opportunities and was pleased to spot a vacancy for a lectureship in international law at the University of Hull, my other alma mater. I contacted my former professors at Hull, who suggested that I submit an application. I was shortlisted, interviewed, and offered the position, which I gratefully accepted. Nearly four years after obtaining my LLM with distinction at Hull, I returned to the university as a lecturer in 1993. This was the start of my career in British academia. To date, I have published 10 books and nearly 60 journal articles that have furthered the knowledge of international law and human rights; I have visited 86 countries to speak at about 200 international conferences; and I have established new academic and other forms of intellectual organisations, both in the UK and abroad. The nature and scope of my publications, and their impact on the lives of people around the globe, on policymaking by governments in different countries, and on the reform agendas of international institutions, are outlined in Chapter 7. This chapter focuses on my personal and professional life as a global citizen in Britain.

Although I was pleased to have gained a foothold in British academia, it quickly dawned on me that I was a latecomer to the field at the age of 34; and, supporting a family of four, the salary at the starting scale of a lecturer seemed too low. Almost half of my take home pay of about £950 per month was swallowed up by the rental costs for our family flat. Also, some students – especially British undergraduates – complained about my Nepalese accent, because at the time they were not used to hearing foreign accents like mine. Quickly, I realised that life in academia would not be quite as rosy as anticipated.

In England in the early 1990s, there were few law lecturers of foreign origin. Linguistic diversity had not yet been embraced. Today, by contrast, the world has become a global village, and British society has become truly multicultural; about one-third of academics in Britain are of foreign origin and the numbers are growing across all disciplines. Students are just as mobile and have an international outlook. However, this was not so much the case yet in 1993, when I began teaching law at Hull. I therefore accepted an offer in July 1993 to teach international law at an international institution of higher education in The Hague. The increase in salary of nearly one-third was most welcome. My new institution was a kind of diplomatic training academy which was fully funded by the Dutch government, and the student population was primarily comprised junior to mid-career diplomats and government law officers from around the globe.

A Highlander's Journey to the Lowlands and Return to the Islands

Our family of four set sail for the Netherlands on an overnight ferry in January 1994, accompanied by all of our belongings, in a state of high anticipation at the prospect of starting out a new life in a new country. When we arrived at our rented apartment in The Hague, some of our neighbours came out to greet us. One asked, 'Bosnie Herzgovini?' At the time, the civil war was raging in former Yugoslavia, the country was breaking apart and many people were fleeing to other European countries, including the Netherlands.

Our lives flourished in The Hague, the mecca of international law. Many foreign diplomats, judges of the International Court of Justice (ICJ), and people working for other international legal institutions, such as the Yugoslavia Tribunal, became friends. My spacious office was located in a stately building close to the ICJ and overlooking the Peace Palace, the home of the court. Within a year of my arrival, I had earned a promotion and had been offered a permanent contract.

We bought a double-boven house – a house in which the living quarters were located upstairs and which had a direct entrance from the street downstairs. Some areas of The Hague are below sea level, and hence global warming and sea level rises were hotly debated. We were probably extra cautious as we were buying our first property in a new country and wanted to secure a safe and stable home. The whole family enjoyed the new house; I thrived in my new job, and we settled in happily to our new lives.

The only issue was the language. Without learning Dutch, we would be unable to integrate well into Dutch society. However, we were living the lives of expats: the medium of instruction at the institute was English; most of my colleagues and friends were also foreign, as were the students; and every Dutch person we encountered spoke to us in English – which was helpful, but not conducive to us learning Dutch. Furthermore, soon after I joined the institute, a senior and very supportive Dutch colleague, Nico Schrijver, asked me to cover some of his teaching so that he could devote more time to completing his PhD. Nico went on to become professor of international law at Leiden University, a senator in the Dutch Parliament, and a member of the Council of State (equivalent to the Privy Council in the UK), and remains a dear family friend to this day. I gladly agreed to take on some of his teaching, so the first year in The Hague flew by without me taking time to attend Dutch language classes.

Unable to speak the language of the country I was living in nor to find the time to learn it, I found myself in a difficult situation. So when the University of Hull offered me a permanent post as a senior lecturer in 1996 to attract me back, we decided to return to the UK. I was also keen to avail of the superb research and publication opportunities that British academia offers: after all, it was primarily to fulfil my ambitions to embark on an academic career in the UK that I had decided to resign from my prestigious government job in Nepal after completing my DPhil.

Thus, in 1996, we returned to Hull, where I strove to improve my English pronunciation by regularly listening to BBC Radio 4 and imitating the broadcasters' manner of speaking. Through my associations with ICJ judges in The Hague, such as Justice Weeramantry and Justice Koroma, I had learned of an unspoken rule at the court: lawyers pleading before the ICJ were meant to speak slowly, a rate of 100 words per minute was the norm. So when delivering my lectures, I deliberately spoke slowly, which helped my students to understand; and in turn, they rated my teaching highly. Meanwhile, my productivity in terms of research output skyrocketed and secured me a series of promotions, from a lectureship in 1993 to professorship within six years, in 1999.

In 2004, I was appointed professor of international law at the University of Leeds. I became the first professor of international law in the history of the university and was tasked with spearheading the internationalisation of its legal curriculum. The university gave me the freedom to develop new international law programmes and to establish a Centre for International Governance, enabling me to put Leeds Law School on the wider global map.

Having now spent half of my working life in Yorkshire, some of my colleagues have bestowed on me the title of 'honorary Yorkshireman'. In 2020, the University of Hull in the East Riding of Yorkshire awarded me an honorary Doctor of Laws (LLD) in recognition of my achievements in the field of international law and human rights. I was delighted to receive such a prestigious accolade from one of my alma maters. I began my academic career at the University of

Hull, and the city played an important role in the formative years of both of my children, who attended the Froebel House School and Hymers College, which provided them with a high-quality education. In those days, the University of Hull attracted iconic figures such as Archbishop Desmond Tutu of South Africa, whose speech left a lasting impression on me and my family.

I had the privilege of meeting Archbishop Desmond Tutu twice during his visits to Hull and of attending the lectures that he delivered during his visit. I still remember with joy the following words from his 1999 Wilberforce Public Lecture:

> I want you to go away from here knowing that we are made for goodness. We are made for beauty. We are made for laughter. We are made for joy. We're made for goodness. We're made for compassion, for gentleness, for sharing.

Archbishop Tutu was a man of vision, courage, and wisdom. The world is poorer for his passing in December 2021.

While we were living in Hull, we also frequently visited the Wilberforce Institute, which is a kind of a public museum named after Yorkshire-born William Wilberforce, renowned for his role in abolishing slavery. In December 2021, I was proud to learn, that the Wilberforce Institute for the Study of Slavery and Emancipation, a research institute at the University of Hull, established an annual prize called 'Professor Subedi Global Essay Prize on Modern Slavery and the Protection of Human Dignity'.

The Hassles of Life as a Global Citizen

Throughout my career, I have spent considerable time travelling the world to visit international universities for research, deliver guest lectures, present papers at conferences, and undertake human rights assignments. Some of the challenges of life as a global citizen and frequent traveller include encounters with immigration and visa officers. Ever since the 9/11 attacks in New York in 2001, I have occasionally found myself in awkward situations due to my busy and far-flung travel itinerary. For instance, after teaching in Suriname for two weeks I was returning to London via Amsterdam when I was almost detained for interrogation by immigration and security personnel at the airports in Amsterdam and London. On my way to board the aircraft in Amsterdam, I was stopped by a security guard who demanded to see my passport. When he spotted the Dutch and British permanent resident permits in my Nepalese passport, he asked me where I lived. I explained that I lived in both England and the Netherlands, as I had been hired to teach a compact part-time course at my previous institution in The Hague during the Easter holidays, but that my main residency was in London. The security guard became increasingly suspicious when he saw my Surinamese visa and said: 'You are Nepalese, but you say you live in both England and the Netherlands – why in two countries? And what were you doing in Suriname?'

Intending to prevent me from boarding the aircraft and interrogate me further, the security guard called his line manager. Fortunately, the line manager seemed more discerning; he examined my passport and asked me what I had been doing in Suriname. He took a closer look at the beautiful bunch of tropical flowers that I had carried all the way from Suriname for Kokila and then told his subordinate to let me board the aircraft: 'He is Nepalese and not from one of the countries on the suspect list, and he is a doctor of law. He is carrying a beautiful bunch of flowers – he must love somebody and his life. Let him go to that person!' Eventually, I was allowed to board the aircraft bound for London.

But more trouble was awaiting me on my arrival at Heathrow. I had been in and out of the UK hundreds of times and had never previously been subjected to a luggage search. This time, however, upon my arrival, two security guards demanded that I open my first suitcase, observing me closely during the process. When they saw the stacks of law books and documents in my suitcase, they quickly allowed me to proceed to the exit, saying that they were not looking for people who were carrying piles of books in their luggage.

On another occasion, in order to travel to Japan to attend a conference, as a Nepalese passport holder I had to visit the Japanese embassy in person to apply for my visa. I had called the embassy in advance to ensure that I had all the necessary papers to process my visa application when I visited the embassy. However, upon my arrival, the desk clerk looked at my Nepalese passport and then asked for an additional letter from my employer, seemingly implying that he did not believe that I was a professor of law in the UK. I was furious, saying: 'I am not trying to enter Japan as a refugee. I have been invited by the University of Tokyo to hold a lecture and to present a paper at a conference'. I showed him the invitation from the University of Tokyo and told him that I felt outraged at the *ad hoc* requirement for an additional letter of confirmation just because I was Nepalese and not British. Following this exchange, the desk clerk went to talk to his superior and as a result I received my visa right away.

A Surprise from the British Government

Fortunately, other encounters with governmental bureaucracies were of a pleasant nature. While busy researching, writing, and publishing in all major areas of international law, one day – much to my delight – I received a letter from the Foreign and Commonwealth Office (FCO) stating that I was to be awarded the title of Honorary Officer of the Order of the British Empire (OBE) for my services to international law and to British–Nepali relations. The press release issued by the FCO on 13 October 2004 announcing the award highlighted the nature of the OBE, my contribution to international law, and my accomplishments. It read in part:

1. British Honours are awarded on merit for exceptional achievement or service to British interests. The Most Excellent Order of the British Empire awards were founded in 1917 to recognise service by civilians in the First World War. The order now honours civilians and service personnel for public service and other distinctions.
2. The honour OBE is that of an Officer of the Most Excellent Order of the British Empire. Honorary awards are conferred by the Queen, on the advice of the Foreign and Commonwealth Secretary, on those foreign nationals who have made an important contribution to British interests. They are made throughout the year and are quite distinct from the New Year and Birthday Honours Lists.

The British government organised a special investiture for me in the India Council Chamber of the FCO on 19 October 2004, and the then British foreign secretary, Jack Straw, delivered the following speech:

> We are here today to honour a very distinguished international lawyer, who has made a great contribution to the United Kingdom's close relationship with the Kingdom of Nepal. The words 'international

law' conjure up images of the United Nations Security Council in session, discussing affairs of war and peace. But international law also regulates a much wider range of human activity – from the WTO rules which govern world trade, to the Air Services Agreements that let aeroplanes fly between countries, to rules governing the use and abuse of the air or the water which nations share. International law is the cement which holds the international structure and relationships together. And the United Kingdom is firmly committed to the rule of law in international relations.

Yes, international law still largely relies on the consent of states; it is broken from time to time; it requires social and political pressure to encourage good behaviour, and sometimes firm action to enforce it. But so, too, does domestic law. International law is not a perfect nor a fully developed instrument. But after millennia in which the relations between states were governed by the balance of force, today we have a framework of rules which apply to all and which underpin the peaceful coexistence and the prosperity of our countries. That is a sure foundation on which to build.

He went on to highlight my contribution to international law and my accomplishments, as follows:

Professor, you have made a highly distinguished contribution to our understanding of international law, and to its evolution. Your work, in publications and in your teaching activities, has spanned almost every aspect of it – with a special focus on issues such as trade, investment, development and the environment, which make a real difference to people's lives. And your career has also been dedicated to advancing international friendship and understanding. You have served your own country, Nepal, with great distinction, including at the United Nations.

Your work on international commissions and committees shows your dedication to putting the principles of the law into practice. And you have been, as it were, an ambassador for Nepal and for Nepal's relationship with Britain in your work in this country – including at the Universities of Hull, London and Middlesex, and now at the University of Leeds, where I myself was privileged to study law in the 1960s.

This honour is in recognition both of your distinction as a lawyer, and of your great contribution to the friendship and partnership between nations, and especially between the United Kingdom

> and the Kingdom of Nepal ... It is in recognition of your valuable services that Her Majesty the Queen has appointed you to be an honorary Officer of the Most Excellent Order of the British Empire. It is with great pleasure that I, on Her Majesty's behalf, present you with the badge of the Order.

I delivered my OBE acceptance speech at the ceremony, which was attended by my family, friends, and colleagues, as well as some prominent British international lawyers, including my Oxford professor Sir Ian Brownlie, and the legal adviser to the FCO Sir Michael Wood. I was delighted to have Professor Brownlie present in the ceremony, as, together with Professor Christine Gray, he was instrumental in helping me to commence an academic career in international law in Britain. The international legal community took pride in my award, and the speech by the British foreign secretary and my acceptance speech were subsequently published in full in the newsletter of the International Law Association (ILA), a leading organisation of international lawyers from around the globe. My OBE for services to international law was a significant award for me personally, as well as for the wider community of international lawyers. In his introductory note to the speeches, the editor of the ILA newsletter states that the award highlights 'the important role of international law in the conduct of international relations'.[1]

The news of my OBE also went viral in Nepal and among the Nepalese diaspora around the globe, as this was the first time that this British state honour had been awarded to a civilian Nepali. Nepal's main national daily newspaper, *Kantipur*, published the story on its front page with my photo above the caption 'The Sun Rose in the West' – a reference to my first name, which is the Nepali word for 'sun'. The newspaper also published my OBE acceptance speech, translated into Nepali. I was touched when I received messages of congratulations not only from colleagues and friends in both Nepal and the UK, but also from people of Nepalese origin all along the northern belt of India, including Dehradun, Darjeeling, and Sikkim. They said that the news of a Nepali being awarded an OBE had brought them joy and pride. I was deeply moved by these messages.

1 ILA Newsletter 2005 No 22, London.

Qualifying as a Barrister in Global Britain

It was while working as a consultant on international legal matters and handling some international law-related cases for a leading London law firm, Mishcon de Reya, that I realised I needed to qualify as a lawyer in the jurisdiction that had become my home. I had qualified as an advocate in Nepal and practised law there, but I had not yet qualified in the UK. I sought to qualify as a barrister, because a barrister's work seemed semi-academic and hence a good fit for me. However, I was already in my mid-forties, had been a full professor of law in England for several years, and had even been awarded an OBE. I therefore resolved to keep a low profile on the barrister training course and planned to sit at the back of the class throughout the duration of the course.

The training programme to qualify as a barrister was very demanding, so I became a full-time student once more. My fellow students were graduates aged 22 or 23, who had just completed the Bar Vocational Course. The practice of law in the UK – especially court procedures and civil and criminal procedures – was completely new to me. In class, we read and role-played cases. One day, the instructor revealed my professional background to the group and from that day on the assumption was that I would lead most group discussions and would have the answers to the most difficult questions. I thus had to work even harder to live up to these expectations.

At times, and particularly in the first few weeks, I was unsure whether to carry on with this endeavour; but I gradually began to enjoy learning the art of advocacy and rose to the challenge. The high-quality teaching and coaching course was offered by the Middle Temple and was taught by some of the best lawyers in the country, including Queen's Counsels (QCs). A few years later, I also completed the public access course run by the Bar Council of England, which allowed me to be instructed directly by members of the public. Once again, my plan to lie low on the course was thwarted: with a name-plate bearing my name and titles placed on my desk, the expectation of my fellow course participants that I would have the answers to even the toughest questions was palpable.

Recently, and especially after the Brexit referendum, there has been a great deal of talk about 'global Britain', and I have given recognition to this phrase in the title of this chapter. To me, 'global Britain' denotes a Britain that promotes multilateralism, free and fair trade, sustainable development and human rights at the international level, and multiculturalism at the domestic level; a Britain, whose politics are underpinned by the values of universalism, tolerance, non-discrimination, and respect for personal liberty. 'Global Britain' also signifies the aspiration is for a kinder, gentler country, whose policies are informed by a positive, outward-looking approach and are designed to enable the UK to become a force for good in the world – whether in promoting democracy, the rule of law and human rights, or in leading the fight against climate change. The UK is a country of laws, and the legal systems of many countries around the world draw on the English common law system. The qualification of a barrister in England is held in high esteem both at home and abroad, and barristers can generally make a decent living as independent practitioners. These were just some of the reasons why I was attracted to the English Bar.

In July 2007, I was admitted to the 'Utter Bar' – that is, called to the Bar – making me a barrister of England and Wales and ready to develop my independent law practice. However, soon after qualifying, I accepted a senior-level appointment within the UN system of human rights and was thus unable to devote the necessary time to build a law practice. I am still glad that I became a student once again in my forties and worked hard to qualify for the English Bar; it has been beneficial in so many ways. I have since realised that the English Bar – and especially the London Bar – offers many opportunities. The main reasons why Britain – and especially London – is such a desirable place to do business and to practise law include the following:

- A trusted legal system and independent judiciary.
- Stable and relatively clean politics.
- A reliable, relatively honest civil service.
- A generally liberal, global outlook among both politicians and the general public.
- Marginalisation of far-right political parties.
- English as a global language.
- The superior quality of broadsheet newspapers and television debates.
- The prominence of global issues both in daily political debate and in general elections.
- The importance afforded to international law, which is greater in Britain than in many other countries.

- Independent schools, grammar schools and world-class universities that provide a high-quality education.
- A vibrant culture.
- The pomp and pageantry of the monarchy.
- Good transportation and communications networks.
- The absence of natural calamities and extreme weather conditions.
- A relatively low crime rate.
- The abundant green spaces of London, which give it the feel of a village amid the hustle and bustle.
- An ideal location in terms of time zone, which allows businesses to engage with each other by telephone or online all across the world.

I realised the advantages of my London location when representing a government client in an international investment arbitration, in collaboration with other teams of counsel based in Hong Kong and Washington DC. While all team meetings took place during regular working hours for me, they meant a very early start for the team in DC and a late night for the Hong Kong-based team.

Becoming a Silk

I was delighted to take silk within ten years of becoming a barrister: in January 2017, the British government announced that Her Majesty the Queen had appointed me as a Queen's Counsel *honoris causa*, in recognition of my contribution to the development of international law and the advancement of human rights. The press release read as follows:

> He is a distinguished academic who has made a major contribution to international law and human rights. He has published extensively in international law and human rights. He served for 5 years between 2010 and 2015 as a member of the Advisory Group on Human Rights to the British Foreign Secretary. During his tenure as UN Special Rapporteur for human rights he produced 4 substantive reports published by the United Nations focusing on judicial, parliamentary, electoral, and land reform in Cambodia. A number of his recommendations were implemented by the government. Collectively, these 4 reports provided an analytical point

> of reference for democracy, human rights and the rule of law in the country and became a primary source of reference for human rights defenders, UN agencies, and donor agencies that continue to be drawn on today. He was awarded an OBE in 2004 for services to international law, and he has continued to make an exceptional contribution over a sustained period at the international level to develop international law and to advance human rights.[2]

I received the news of my appointment through the media while holidaying in Malta and was thrilled to be awarded the highest legal title that can be given to a lawyer in the UK.

On 13 February 2017, the lord chancellor of the UK formally conferred me with the title of QC in a grand formal ceremony in Westminster Hall. For this once-in-a-lifetime event, I hired a formal morning suit – a long tailcoat with top hat – bought a silk tie and booked an executive-style, chauffeur-driven black Mercedes Benz C class car to travel with my family to the Palace of Westminster, where Dr Chris Staker and Dr James Busuttil, who have been friends since our DPhil days at Oxford, my former pupillage master, Richard Nowinski, and the head clerk at Three Stone Chambers, Justin Brown, joined us in the celebrations.

The Palace of Westminster looked beautiful and bright in the crisp morning light. Silks, judges, and their guests had gathered in Westminster Hall, which was buzzing with cheerful, lively conversations. I felt proud as my family and I joined the crowd. The ceremony began in style at exactly 11:00 am with the procession of the lord chancellor, who went on to deliver a highly complimentary speech congratulating the five new honorary QCs, whom she hailed as 'the best and brightest of the legal profession of the best legal system in the world'. We were then called forward one by one to take our oath of allegiance before the lord chancellor and be conferred with the title of QC and handed our letters patent of appointment from Her Majesty the Queen.

Upon receiving the letter of appointment, we were ushered to the top of the steps of the hall for a formal group photograph of all the newly

2 The full citation for the award of this title is available in a British government press release: www.gov.uk/government/news/lord-chancellor-welcomes-historic-promotion-of-talent-for-new-silks.

appointed QCs. The sun was streaming through the large stained-glass windows illuminating the magnificent hall, built for the courts that had once sat before they moved to the current building of the Royal Courts of Justice. After the formal proceedings, Kokila, Anita, my friends and I headed to the restaurant in the vault of the Royal Society of Arts on the Strand, where fellow diners who spotted the insignia of my OBE on the lapel of my morning suit and the red-leather wallet of my QC appointment letter on the table, approached us to pass on their congratulations. Throughout the day we missed Pranay, who was unable to attend due to a job interview with a new private equity firm in London. Much to our delight, however, all of my family and more friends came together at the reception in the Grand Hall of my Inn, the Middle Temple, to celebrate the award, later that year.

My honorary QC was the first ever conferred on an international lawyer; hence, I have made legal history in England. Usually, the title is conferred on individuals who have made an outstanding contribution to an area of municipal law or the law of England. The award sparked interest in the field of international law, and I received letters of congratulations from leading international lawyers, judges, and arbitrators from around the globe, including the president of the ICJ, Judge Hishashi Owada; Justice Lord Jonathan Mance of the UK Supreme Court and president of the ILA; Justice Peter Tomka of the ICJ; Professor Vaughan Lowe of the University of Oxford; Professor Alain Pellet, president of the French Society of International Law; and celebrated international lawyer and top US arbitrator Professor Charles Brower. Professor Tommy Koh, a diplomat and fellow international lawyer of Singapore, wrote a message of congratulations in which he said that I had done the whole of Asia proud. I was also touched to receive congratulations from Cherie Blair QC, a leading lawyer in the UK and the wife of former Prime Minister Tony Blair, who sent me a note after reading the news of my appointment in *Counsel* magazine, the flagship journal of the Bar Council of England.

While QCs are commonly associated with affluence, this does not apply to me. I consider myself a scholar, and my academic work has remained my main occupation. Furthermore, shortly after I became a barrister, I was appointed as the special rapporteur for human rights in Cambodia by the UN, a post which I was to hold for the next six years. I observed in an interview with *Counsel* magazine that although there is a degree of overlap between the work of a legal academic and a barrister, academics 'go one step further and ask what is wrong with the law and what ought to be changed'. This is what I have done through my publications in international law; but this may not be so conducive to the role of a barrister. In my opinion, successful barristers and QCs are exceptionally skilled craftspeople with the neutral stance necessary to engage governments in cases before international courts and tribunals, or to appoint them as an arbitrator. QCs usually analyse and explain the law, and hone their understanding of law and legal argumentation, rather than critiquing the law and expressing their views on its fairness or pointing to the need for reforms.

By contrast, through my extensive research into international law, I have exposed gaps and weaknesses in the law itself – and frequently also in the practice of law – and have proposed changes to promote a fair and stable international community based on solid principles of international law. It may thus appear to some that I am rather an opinionated law academic than a neutral barrister, which could have hindered my success at the English and international Bar. However, I set out to study and practise law to make a tangible, positive difference to the lives of others around the globe, and I am proud of my achievements in doing so.

Appointment as an Adviser to the British Foreign Secretary

One of the ways in which I feel I have made such a tangible difference is through my appointment as a member of the Advisory Group on Human Rights to the British foreign secretary in 2010. While I had been appointed by Her Majesty the Queen as the crown representative on the governing board of SOAS University of London in 2007, this was my first major government post in the UK and an opportunity for me to contribute to top-level policymaking. My appointment was announced in Parliament in a ministerial note.

It was an honour and a pleasure to work with the then British foreign secretary, William Hague, and other members of the Advisory Group on Human Rights on various projects aimed at promoting and protecting human rights globally, especially in countries where human rights violations were a major cause for international concern. I came to know Hague as a keen intellectual and an erudite person. He had authored two superb books: one on William Wilberforce, who was instrumental in abolishing slavery; and one on William Pitt the Younger, the youngest prime minister of Britain. I also relished the opportunity to collaborate with other esteemed friends and international law colleagues on the advisory group, such as Professor Sir Malcolm Evans and Professor Chaloka Beyani. I believe that we strengthened human rights and improved the lives of many people in strife-torn countries through our work, thus enhancing Britain's reputation as a force for good.

My work as an adviser to the British foreign secretary also afforded me a glimpse into the inner workings of some parts of the British government, which gave me insight into the nature of the influence and limitations of British soft power in the international arena. Invitations to various high-level diplomatic receptions in grand British hospitality venues such as Lancaster House in London provided spice to my life as a government adviser and the opportunity to interact with London-based foreign ambassadors from all around the world. My five years in this position allowed me to put my theoretical academic knowledge into practice. In addition to the foreign secretary, a number of other ministers interacted with our advisory group and sought our advice.

The role of government adviser presents mutual advantages to both parties – minister and adviser. The ministers benefited from our subject expertise while we benefited from their current thinking and policies they were considering. Ministers sought our advice on proposed measures, and we learned of some government plans and decisions much earlier than anyone else. Where necessary, we asked ministers and their subordinates difficult questions – which William Hague especially never eschewed, as he valued alternative perspectives. We did not support every decision and proposal that ministers put forward, and frequently criticised government policy and activities. Our role as advisers essentially involved contributing to, critically assessing, and providing input on government decisions and policymaking on human rights. While acknowledging our work, the ministers did not necessarily follow our advice, of course. I nonetheless valued these exclusive insights into the challenges faced by ministers and their (often different) perspectives on these matters.

Multiculturalism and Racism

My experiences in the UK have led me to believe that my nationality has been no obstacle to success. Admittedly, at the start of my career, I sometimes found it difficult to compete with home-grown colleagues and to succeed on foreign turf; yet I soon felt that I had become a native in Europe and especially in global Britain. I no longer thought of myself as a foreigner in the UK. The QC and DCL titles, and especially the OBE, caused me to feel both most British and most Nepali at once. In pursuit of my academic career, based in the UK, I have travelled the world for research projects, conferences, and visiting professorships; and in doing so I have sampled the world's diverse cultures. In Sanskrit, we say 'beer bhogya basundhara', meaning that those who are brave get to enjoy all the earthly things that are on offer. I am now inclined to add 'biddwan bhogya basundhara', meaning that those who work in British academia can also enjoy all the earthly things on offer.

Raising our children in the UK and taking great interest in their activities has also helped to make me feel at home here. We exposed our children to a wide variety of extracurricular activities, from ballet to Beavers and Scouts and courses run by the British Red Cross. Both Pranay and Anita took to music and played the piano and violin. Pranay enjoyed cricket at school and played at our local Elizabethan cricket club in Barnet, which gave us the opportunity to enjoy picnics at the side of the cricket ground together with other families.

Having lived and worked in several European countries and the US, my view is that Britain is a liberal, tolerant, inclusive, and multicultural country. Naturally, people with racist views reside in many countries in the world, including the UK. The kinds of racist perceptions and the degree of racist hostilities clearly vary; crucially, governmental policies restrict their expression. Fortunately, neither my family nor I have ever been subjected to racially motivated assaults, whether verbal or physical. UK universities are working hard to combat racism; hence, it may well be that my profession has spared me the experiences of racism reported by people in other walks of life in Britain.

In my line of work, I have encountered many individuals of foreign origin who changed their ethnic name or identity in a bid to assimilate more easily into UK society and progress in their careers. I decided to embrace the UK and the world as who I was: a Vedic Nepali with an ethos of universalism, secularism, tolerance, respect for personal liberty, and the belief that the world is one family. I came to the UK to work and live at the invitation of a prestigious university and never felt that I was a foreigner here. Coming from a country with 5,000 years of unbroken Hindu-Buddhist heritage, which had never been colonised by a foreign power, I never felt inferior in any sense in Britain and never held grievances of any kind against anyone. During my formative years in Nepal, I learned from the Mahabharata that one should never undermine oneself, underestimate one's ability, or consider oneself small or inferior.

I have never regarded myself as a member of an ethnic or minority community in the UK, such as the black, Asian, and minority ethnic (BAME) community. I identify as a global citizen and never considered myself defined by a narrow social label. Other people, of course, may view me as 'BAME' without my wish or consent. I have never joined any ethnic, minority, or BAME-related societies, whether socially or professionally.

Subtle and unconscious racist bias is difficult to pinpoint, and a degree of prejudice against people from other backgrounds exists in most societies. One of our former neighbours in the UK – a well-educated, liberal person whose parents had immigrated to the UK from Eastern Europe – inadvertently implied during a friendly chat that he was British, whereas I was a foreigner. When I politely reminded him that the only difference between us was that he was a second-generation immigrant and I was a first-generation immigrant, he realised his mistake and apologised.

When I recently asked my children whether they had experienced any racism in the UK, they both said they had not; Pranay went on to suggest, 'You have to look for it to find racism here'. This reminded me of a statement by Colin Powell, chief of the American defence staff and later secretary of state, who said: 'Racism may be interested in me, but I am not interested in racism'. 'Namaste', meaning 'I bow to the divine within you', is used in Nepal and in most of the Hindu and Buddhist world as a greeting. It signifies the nature of my engagement with people, since I see the divine qualities within each human being beyond their appearance. During difficult encounters in particular, I am less interested in the person's words and external demeanour, and pay close attention to their internal conflicts and motivations, which helps to foster a respectful connection and mutual exchange.

Although I myself tick the 'Hindu' box on forms that list religions, in truth I don't identify as a Hindu. The ancient Greeks and Romans bestowed the name 'Hindu' on the people living in the Indus Valley and in the Indus and Ganges river basins. By birth and orientation, I am a Vedic or Vedi – a follower of the Vedas, the ancient Hindu scriptures. The original spelling of my surname is 'Suvedi', rather than the slightly altered 'Subedi', meaning a follower of the Vedas or those who have mastered the Vedas. Traditionally, a Vedic or Vedi is someone who engages in activities to enhance his spirituality, acquires knowledge and wisdom, and shares it with other people by teaching or advising in policymaking. Thus, Britain has provided me with abundant opportunities to live up to my name and my religion, for which I am immensely grateful.

Over the years, British academia has witnessed phenomenal growth in academic diversity. Thanks to the internet, all academic vacancies and opportunities in the UK are advertised across the globe, and the most talented candidates from around the world compete for academic and research positions in Britain. Consequently, about one-third of academics and researchers in British academia are now of foreign origin, and this number continues to grow across all disciplines. The demographic picture of the student population is likewise changing: foreign students represent nearly 50% of the postgraduate cohort in any given academic year at most British universities, and the number of female students has overtaken the number of male students in many disciplines, such as law. It has been a pleasure for me to teach the diverse, ambitious, and talented young people now studying at British universities. I recall attending one PhD examination at a British university that was a particularly striking reflection of this diversity: the candidate was Mexican; his supervisor was Pakistani; the external examiner (me) was Nepalese; the internal examiner was an Indian of Kenyan origin; the person chairing the exam was a Briton of Irish origin; and the university and the degree were British. This is how the landscape of British academia has changed thanks to the dynamics of our increasingly globalised world.

London Life

Although I have worked at the University of Leeds since 2004, Kokila and I decided to base our principal residence in Barnet, North London – mainly to further our children's education. While Barnet is a town, it has a pastoral feel, with its hills and woodlands, which is why I call it 'Rurbania' – a blend of the rural and the urban. This has meant I have had to commute to my post in Leeds, which has been an acceptable compromise.

As I see it, the family is the smallest unit of democracy. The decisions on our home moves – from Nepal to Oxford, Oxford to The Hague, The Hague to Hull, and Hull to London – were thus taken after rounds of consultations with the family and by majority vote. So too were all other crucial life decisions, from the academic subjects that our children would pursue, to the universities they would choose. This even extended to whether to support Leave or Remain in the Brexit referendum: I initially leaned towards Leave, but after many discussions with the family, I was persuaded to switch my support to Remain. We provided our children with the best education we could, and they have become intellectual friends and advisers as a result. In the Brexit debate around our family dinner table, they presented their submissions powerfully and I submitted to their views. Anita is the more talented lawyer in the family, and I keep losing out to her in our most controversial discussions.

Meanwhile, living in London has allowed me to attend numerous events at the embassy of Nepal, at which successive ambassadors have introduced me to their circles of diplomats. The embassy hosted a celebratory event when I was appointed QC and again when I was awarded the Oxford DCL. One year in May, when getting ready for the ceremony at the embassy to celebrate Republic Day, Nepal's national day, I put on all of my medals and decorations as requested in the invitation, including my OBE and the three state honours awarded to me by the monarchs of Nepal. When Anita saw me in my regalia, she said: 'Dad, you look like a Christmas tree with so many decorations, and a Christmas tree out of season does not go down well'. Pranay suggested that the idea was to inspire people and that my medals and decorations should serve this purpose. At the ceremony, many guests asked to have their photographs taken with me and enquired about my medals. Mr Alan Duncan – the minister of the Department for International Development and the chief guest at the ceremony – even jested, 'I envy you!' The sentiment was short-lived, as later that year he received a knighthood.

When I turned 60 and qualified for a free travel pass in London, I momentarily contemplated retirement, but realised that my academic drive was as strong as ever. I have since written two more books, one of which – *Human Rights in Eastern Civilisations* – featured in an article on my life and work published in April 2021 in *Counsel* magazine. The article entitled 'Legal Personality – The International Human Rights Jurist: Surya Subedi QC', written by Admas Habteslasie, a fellow barrister from another set of chambers in London, charted the journey of my career and explored the way in which I combined an academic career with more practical work in the field of public international law and with contributions to top-level policy formulation within and outside of the UN system of human rights.

Upon learning of this article, the University of Leeds published a story about it, to celebrate the fact that one of its law professors had been featured in this way in the prestigious magazine of a professional national legal institution of England and Wales. This was all a source of great pride and satisfaction for me, my family, and my colleagues, both in Leeds and at my chambers in London.

The article – which captured the essence of a lifetime spent working in different capacities both in Britain and abroad, including in my native Nepal and Cambodia – inspired me to write this memoir. I would disagree with the English writer Quentin Crisp's characterisation of a memoir as 'an obituary in serial form with the last instalment missing'. I am confident that there will be other exciting chapters in my life before the last instalment comes, as I consider myself to be in my prime in my youthful early sixties and am relishing the freedom associated with this.

Hopeful Times

As someone with a rebellious mind from early on in life, I have cherished the academic freedom that I have enjoyed in the UK. I research, publish, and teach on all areas of international law and travel the globe researching and teaching global values. In short, I am doing the work of a pukka Brahmin in England.

I value the outstanding education that Britain's world-class universities offer and I am proud to be a part of it. British universities attract talent from all around the globe and have long served as crucibles of knowledge. The law schools up and down the country – including my own at the University of Leeds – are in the business of producing not only lawyers, but also future leaders of society, both national and international.

When I travel abroad, people ask me how I would define Britain. My response is always that it is a country of laws, and is rooted in the principles of the rule of law, democracy, human rights, tolerance, and fair play. Britain has spearheaded the endeavours to promote the rule of law at the international level – not least through its contributions to the drafting of the European Convention on Human Rights and the Rome Statute of the International Criminal Court (ICC). It is one of a handful of major powers which has both accepted the compulsory jurisdiction of the ICJ and ratified the Rome Statute of the ICC. Britain has been progressive in advancing the rule of law internationally and the values of the international community embedded therein, as well as the role of the British judiciary.

I am pleased to call Britain my home, as fairness and meritocracy run deep in the society. It is said that Britain is a country where you can be anything you want to be, and my experiences as recounted in this memoir would bear this out.

4 Contribution to Democracy and Human Rights in Cambodia

The Sounds, Sights, and Scents of Asia

On 25 March 2009, the UN Human Rights Council unanimously endorsed my nomination by the president of the council to be the new UN special rapporteur for human rights in Cambodia – which at the time was one of only 12 country rapporteur positions in the UN system. On 14 June 2009, I departed on my first fact-finding mission to Cambodia, and on the way stopped over at the new Suvarnabhumi Airport (whose name translates as 'the land of gold') in Bangkok; as I took in the sounds, sights, and scents of Asia, I immediately felt at ease.

Upon arrival in Phnom Penh, I was led through the VIP lounge to a waiting UN car, which took me to my hotel. I met with the foreign minister of Cambodia on my second day in the country. Much to my surprise, that same day Prime Minister Hun Sen announced in the media that 'the new UN human rights envoy is welcome to Cambodia, but I hope he will not be as ignorant as his predecessor'.[1] I met the prime minister on 18 June for a two-hour discussion of human rights issues in the country.

Throughout our conversation I was under the impression that the prime minister was trying to throw me off course by implying that the chief of the UN high commissioner's field office in Phnom Penh was not conducting himself as an independent, objective, and impartial person in discharging his responsibilities, and that I should report back to the high commissioner in Geneva and the UN secretary-general in New York so

1 Cheang Sokha and Georgia Wilkins, 'U.N. Envoy Welcomed, Warned', *Phnom Penh Post*, 17 June 2009, www.phnompenhpost.com/national/un-envoywelcomed-warned.

DOI: 10.4324/9781003271543-4

as to have him recalled. Apparently, the prime minister had been irked by the firm stand that the field office chief was taking on human rights issues in the country and therefore was seeking to have him replaced. I refused to take the bait. At a press conference held the day before my departure from Cambodia, I outlined my goals in a constructive manner, aware that while a hard-hitting statement might make an immediate impact, it might not serve my purpose in the long run. Some of my predecessors had had the door slammed in their face and so I made an effort to keep the communication channels open.

When I travelled to Cambodia for my second fact-finding mission, in February 2010, I met with Prime Minister Hun Sen in his luxurious, modern office situated in the new building of the Office of the Prime Minister. I was given a lavish welcome and walked a red carpet all the way through the grand foyer to the meeting room of the prime minister. Our meeting, however, did not go well. The prime minister came across as more rigid than before and the atmosphere between us was tense. A meeting with Mr Om Yieng Teng – the president of the Cambodian Human Rights Committee and a senior government minister – followed, which turned out to be even more stressful. He was rather rude to me personally and was angry about my criticisms of Cambodia's human rights record. I realised then that country special rapporteurs must have a sharp mind and a thick skin, as they are often vilified by the government both in person and through the local state media.

Judicial Reform

As a lawyer by training and profession, I began my work by examining the effectiveness of the Cambodian judiciary in protecting people's rights. I examined its ability to deliver justice and to command the respect, trust, and confidence of the people. After conducting two fact-finding visits to Cambodia, I identified a number of shortcomings in the functioning of the judiciary and made recommendations to address them. I stated in my report that the judiciary was not as independent as it should be.

Prime Minister Hun Sen was not pleased about my report and told me to my face on my third visit to the country that, while I was more diplomatic and friendlier than my predecessors, I was no different from them in delivering hard messages. 'You are an old whisky in a new bottle!' he said. I replied: 'Your Excellency, whether it is me or someone else, if we work as the UN special rapporteur for the country, the message will be the same unless and until the situation improves'. With no effective opposition, the UN agencies were muzzled and non-governmental organisations (NGOs) intimidated into silence. I was the only person in Cambodia at the time to speak up for human rights.

Upon completing my third fact-finding mission, I held a press conference to share my assessment of the human rights situation in the country. Furthermore, I issued a press statement entitled 'Criticism is not a crime, but an act of intelligence', in which I expressed that the Cambodian national institutions responsible for upholding people's rights were not as independent as they should be. The press statement received significant coverage in the national and international media the following day. From that point onwards, the Cambodian government turned against me and I started to receive abusive emails, perhaps from supporters of the prime minister. I was not worried or surprised by this development, as I understood from the beginning that in doing human rights work one exposes oneself to insults, threats, and abuses from the agents of autocrats.

When my initial two-year UN mandate was about to expire, the UN Human Rights Council unanimously passed a resolution to renew my mandate for two more years. The mandate of the country special rapporteur is of such a nature that the relevant government does its utmost to abolish it, while the opposition parties, human rights defenders and other civil society organisations all wish it to continue; and the situation in Cambodia was no exception. After the vote, the UK ambassador to the United Nations in Geneva came to see me to offer his congratulations and jokingly asked: 'What is it about you, professor? You are criticising the government of Cambodia, but then they agree to renew your mandate for two more years?' 'It is the art of diplomacy that I learned in the UK', I replied. In fact, Cambodia did not have enough votes on the Council to abolish the mandate; the key players on the Council valued my work and I had not burned all my bridges with the Cambodian government.

Land Rights

Soon after I had commenced my mission in Cambodia, I realised that the manner in which the authorities treated those on the margins of society, the urban poor and indigenous communities, was haphazard. There were no formal national guidelines on land evictions. Although there seemed to be some politicisation of eviction issues, and some of the problems may have been created by land-grabbers and land speculators, many evictions by the authorities were rather heavy-handed, favouring the rich at the expense of the poor. The government was slow in distributing land titles to possible owners and quick in evicting them from sites designated for development, regardless of whether they held possession rights under the law.

The issues associated with land rights disputes and evictions were the most pressing human rights problems in Cambodia as far as ordinary citizens were concerned, and dominated the headlines in the media, both nationally and internationally. The manner in which land was managed and used by the government for various purposes remained a major cause for concern. Land grabbing by those in positions of power was a common occurrence. During my fact-finding missions in the country, delegation after delegation, large and small, comprising members from some of the most vulnerable sections of society, including women and the elderly, came to see me with their petitions, urging me to intervene to protect their land rights. The issues they raised related to land concessions, including forced evictions, poorly planned resettlement and relocation, environmental destruction, unsustainable exploitation of natural resources, and threats to indigenous peoples' livelihood, culture, and traditions. Notably, most of the campaigns for land rights in Cambodia were led by women who were risking or were already being subjected to intimidation, harassment, and arrest by the government.

An increasing number of cases came to my attention in which activists, human rights defenders, individuals and communities who sought to claim their rights to land, had been harassed, threatened, or criminalised for protesting against the granting and management of flawed economic and other land concessions. Consequently, I decided to focus two of my missions on land and housing rights in general, and the human rights impact of economic land concessions in particular. After conducting an extensive fact-finding mission which focused on the human rights impact of economic land concessions, I submitted a detailed report analysing the breadth, depth, and gravity of the issues, and making a series of recommendations to improve the situation. This report on the human rights impact of economic land concessions was welcomed by Cambodia's development partners and wider society. And while the Cambodian government initially criticised some of my conclusions on the true impact of the economic land concessions on the people of Cambodia, it eventually appreciated my report on the whole and started to implement some of my recommendations.

The plight of the people who were being forcibly evicted from their lands and homes in Phnom Penh's Boeung Kak Lake and elsewhere, to make way for foreign commercial developers, was finally being addressed by the government, and compromises were achieved. This was an immense source of relief for me. When my UN role came to an end, some of the memorable events organised to bid me farewell and thank me for my work were held by people whose rights had been violated due to land evictions. The brave women of Cambodia, and especially from Boeung Kak Lake, were those leading the fight for their rights; their appreciation of my work will remain forever in my memory and their farewell gifts occupy pride of place in my heart and in my home.

Electoral Reform

The Constitution of Cambodia establishes the country as a liberal democracy, and elections are central to democracy. However, during my fact-finding missions, I frequently heard allegations of irregularities and systemic problems that undermined the country's ability to hold free and fair elections. I carried out my own independent assessment of the situation, on the basis of which I concluded that reforms were needed to ensure that elections in Cambodia were free and fair, and that Cambodians could exercise their right to democratic governance in a free political environment. I stated in my report on electoral reform that free and fair elections could take place only when there was a free political environment and people could exercise their rights and freedoms, such as the freedom of expression and assembly, as well as the freedom to stand for election. To hold credible elections, the government must ensure high standards in line with its international human rights obligations before, during and after the casting of votes. It must also ensure the independence of the National Election Committee.

I pulled no punches in stating that there were major flaws in the administration of elections in Cambodia, and urgent and longer-term reforms were needed to give Cambodians confidence in the electoral process and in the workings of the National Election Committee. Accordingly, I made a series of recommendations for electoral reform. The main one was to grant constitutional, independent, and autonomous status to the National Election Committee. My key recommendations were as follows:

- The National Election Committee should have independent and autonomous status in the constitutional and legal structure of Cambodia, with its own independent budget allocated by the Parliament. The president and members of the committee should be drawn from a pool of retired senior judges, senior and distinguished members of the Cambodian bar, and senior professors of law, politics, and public administration.
- There should be consensus among the major political parties represented in the Parliament on the appointment of the president and members of the National Election Committee and the provincial election committees. The president and members of the National Election Committee and the provincial election committees should be appointed for a fixed term and have security of tenure. They should be barred from holding positions in political parties during and up to two years after the expiry of their terms of office. All major political parties should have fair and equal access to the mass media to convey their messages to the electorate. The government should ensure that civil servants, police, and military personnel do not participate in political activities or use government resources for party-political purposes while working in their official capacities, and that neutrality is paramount.
- The leader of the opposition should be allowed to return to the country from his exile in France to participate in the political process in the country; this was especially crucial in the run-up to the general elections.

Once I had submitted my report on electoral reform with the above recommendations, I faced the wrath of the government once more. Prime Minister Hun Sen was particularly infuriated by my finding that the National Election Committee was not as independent as it should be.

Personal Attacks

My report on electoral reform created a major stir in Cambodia and the prime minister launched personal attacks against me – as he had done against my predecessor, Professor Yash Ghai, a person of formidable intellect. Attacking me publicly, Prime Minister Hun Sen said that I came from a country which had destroyed its monarchy and had no constitution, and implied that I had no right to criticise Cambodia's human rights record.[2] I published a calm, factual response in all major newspapers in Cambodia. I did not wish to have a public spat with the prime minister. I was aware that every country has its pride and I did not wish to say anything that would dent the pride of Cambodia. I said in my response that I was working in Cambodia in my professional capacity as the UN special rapporteur and was not representing Nepal. I was an independent expert working on behalf of the UN with a view to helping the people of Cambodia. The foreign ambassadors based in Phnom Penh and the UN officials agreed with the way I handled the issue. The head of the UN Development Programme Office in Phnom Penh, Douglas Broderick, wrote to me saying:

> I must say that the classy and extraordinary letter, which was in today's *Cambodia Daily*, page 26 is incredible. There has been a positive feedback from some about your letter. I am proud to work with you along with learning about such extraordinary craftmanship and politeness which helps all of us.[3]

However, Prime Minister Hun Sen now refused to meet me and seemed to have issued orders to all of his ministers not to meet with me either. He again criticised me publicly during my next visit to the country. I remained focused on monitoring the situation of human rights in the country and interacting with other stakeholders in society. On the last day of this latest visit, I ended up giving an impromptu speech in the street to a big crowd of about 300–400 people outside my UN office in Phnom Penh. The crowd had gathered to support

2 Agence France-Presse 'Cambodia PM Hits Out at Critical UN Envoy', *AFP*, 4 October 2012.

3 This letter is on file with the author.

me and to present their own complaints of violations of their rights by the government.

A Low Point in Cambodia

Irked by my report on electoral reform, the government orchestrated two demonstrations against my work during my visit to the country in 2012. Tuk-tuk drivers had been hired by the government to position themselves outside my office and hurl abuse at me. Furthermore, I was ambushed at an event at Mekong Cambodia University, where I had agreed to deliver a lecture. Members of the youth brigade of the ruling Cambodian People's Party unfolded banners saying 'UN Special Rapporteur Go Home', 'Cambodia Does Not Need Professor Subedi', and 'The UN Special Rapporteur Is Undermining Cambodia's Sovereignty'. They even started shouting out these slogans in the lecture theatre. This harassment was a scary experience. Concerned for my safety and wellbeing, US Ambassador Bill Todd later visited me in my hotel and advised me to have a food taster to avoid being poisoned in Cambodia. Before he left, he said that my work was vital to create a better future for the people in the country. After the government-orchestrated protests, the UN provided me with plainclothes UN security staff and advised me not to venture out of the hotel on my own.

At this point, Cambodia's state machinery was also deployed against me: public insults were broadcast on state television and none of my activities were reported. James Heenan, the head of the UN Office of the United Nations High Commissioner for Human Rights (OHCHR) in Phnom Penh, remarked that he was most impressed by my calmness in the face of adversity. Many foreign ambassadors based in Phnom Penh supported me, saying that my work in the country was valuable and change was coming. Moreover, the hostility towards my work galvanised the youth of Cambodia into action: they condemned the government's actions and posted messages of support for me on social media.

This level of political engagement in political affairs acted as a catalyst for large demonstrations demanding change in the country, which nearly toppled the government. The day I left Cambodia, after holding a press conference, the *Cambodia Daily* published on its front page a comprehensive report on the press conference, along with a photo of me. That was its way of supporting me and thanking me for my work; I was touched. The UN security personnel escorted me all the way to the door of the aircraft.

The international community rallied around my recommendations for electoral reform in the country. While making the first-ever visit by a US president to Cambodia in November 2012 to attend the US-Association of South East Asian Nations (ASEAN) summit meeting in Phnom Penh, President Obama called Cambodia's lack of respect for fundamental freedoms an 'impediment' to deeper relations between the two countries, adding that countries that do not uphold certain universal principles, such as respect for human rights, will have more difficulty integrating with the international community. It was reported in the media that President Obama urged the prime minister to implement my recommendations for political reform.[4] Similarly, the European Parliament, the Inter-Parliamentary Union (an inter-governmental organisation of national parliaments of 162 countries),[5] and the Senates of Australia[6] and the Philippines[7] passed resolutions calling on the Cambodian government to implement my recommendations. The main opposition party in Cambodia also threatened to boycott the forthcoming parliamentary elections if my recommendations were not implemented. Nevertheless, the general elections in July 2013 went ahead without the implementation of some of my proposals for electoral reform.

However, the leader of the opposition was allowed to return to the country from exile in France as I had recommended. This permission, unfortunately, was granted too late for him to lead the opposition party in the elections in an effective manner. Still, it was rumoured that the opposition party had actually won the elections, but the National Election Committee had nonetheless declared the ruling party the winner. The opposition party consequently refused to accept the results and started a campaign of protests which quickly gained momentum and received widespread

4 'Rapporteur Backed: Rights or a Rough Ride, Warns U.S.', *Phnom Penh Post* (14 December 2012); 41 2014 OJ (C 72) 6.

5 Governing Council of the Inter-Parliamentary Union [IPU], 191st Sess, CMBD/01 (24 October 2012), www.ipu.org/hr-e/191/cmbd01.htm.

6 Commonwealth, Senate Daily Summary, 29 October 2012, 3152 (Austl).

7 S Res 130, 15th Cong (2012) (Phil).

support. Alleging electoral irregularities in the July 2013 general election and challenging the independence of the National Election Committee, the opposition party members refused to take their oath of office to join Parliament, and took to the streets.

Averting Political Violence

As the world prepared to celebrate the New Year, the scale of the demonstrations in Cambodia increased, resulting in violence. I was in regular contact with UN human rights offices in both Phnom Penh and Geneva, and was closely monitoring the rapidly evolving political situation. When five people were killed in clashes with the police and military police, I had to act fast and issued a statement that very day to put the government on notice and in the international spotlight. Thankfully, with Cambodia being seven to eight hours ahead of UK time, I had just enough time to receive and verify the relevant information and to digest and respond to it. My statement was quickly picked up by national and international media, including CNN and the BBC. I also called the Cambodian ambassador in Geneva to express my deep concern and asked him to convey this to his government in Phnom Penh.

It was on 4 January 2014 – at 4:00 pm UK time and around midnight in Phnom Penh – that the leader of the opposition, Mr Sam Rainsy, called me from Cambodia to inform me that he and his deputy, Mr Khem Sokha, had received a summons to appear in court. He said that they had taken refuge at the French embassy in Phnom Penh and urged me to intervene. He sounded frightened for his life, as attempts had been made on his life before. I reassured him that I would do my best and would visit Cambodia to see the prime minister as soon as possible.

Given the scale of the violence, the number of deaths in the streets of Phnom Penh and the imminent threat of detention of the leader of the opposition, I prepared to fly to Cambodia and informed the UN of my impending visit. The UN Human Rights Office in Geneva warned me that I was risking my personal safety. Much to my surprise, just before my departure from London, I received a letter from the government in Cambodia saying that the prime minister, together with more or less the entire cabinet, would meet with me, given the gravity of the situation in the country. Five people had been killed; scores of people were reported missing; 23 people had been arrested and held incommunicado in a remote prison; and the leaders of the opposition were facing the threat of arrest and prosecution on politically motivated charges.

When I reached Phnom Penh, a large number of people came to see me with a petition. The opposition party requested me to act as a mediator to resolve the political deadlock in the country. I had a meeting with the prime minister and most of his cabinet colleagues for three and a half hours in the main meeting hall of the Council of Ministers. During this meeting, I was bolder, more candid, and more decisive in my argumentation than ever before in delivering my message and concerns to the prime minister. I stated that the government's actions did not meet the test of proportionality, legality, and necessity. The prime minister looked shaken and asked me whether I wanted him to resign. I was surprised by this remark from a man who was known as the 'strongman' of Cambodia and had been in power for a long time. I replied that I was not seeking his resignation; the decision to resign or not was his alone. But his government had to operate within certain norms and implement my recommendations for political reform.

Eager to leverage this opportunity of a meeting with the prime minister and his key cabinet members, I was anxious to make clear in no uncertain terms what was wrong with the present system of governance and what remedial actions were needed. I felt relieved when the prime minister agreed during the meeting to implement many of my recommendations relating to judicial, electoral, and other political reform. The prime minister asked me to convey a message of reconciliation to the leaders of the opposition, which I gladly did. As a result, I spent most of my time during this visit to Cambodia in January 2014 mediating the political reconciliation. I felt vindicated and elated by this chance to contribute to a fairer political system in Cambodia. After various rounds of consultations, on 22 July 2014, the leaders of the ruling party and of the opposition struck a deal to end the political deadlock, which included a commitment to carrying out the electoral reforms that I had recommended.[8]

8 Office of the UN High Commissioner for Human Rights, Cambodia, press release, 'UN Human Rights Expert Hails Political Breakthrough, Calls for Promised Reforms' (22 July 2014), www.ohchr.org/EN/NewsEvents/Pages/DisplayNews.aspx?NewsID=14892&LangID=E.

The leader of the opposition in Cambodia wrote to me on 6 August 2014, saying:

> I want to thank you for your guidance, especially over the last twelve months. Without your insightful recommendations and your discreet and tactful intervention, Cambodia wouldn't have seen this end to the political crisis. However, a historic challenge still lies ahead. To ensure the success of a difficult but necessary reform process in the key sectors you have addressed in your reports Cambodians from all political affiliations need your constant support and that of the United Nations.[9]

Prior to this, he had written to me on 9 June 2014, stating that he deeply appreciated my 'continuous effort to promote democracy and defend human rights in Cambodia. The Khmer people are very lucky to have a friend like you'.[10]

Of course, I experienced periods of despair when the leader of the opposition was exiled in France due to politically motivated charges; when a prominent human rights activist and director of an independent radio station was imprisoned; when attempts to silence dissents from many quarters were made by any means, including assassinations; and when I myself was subjected to orchestrated harassment. However, I remained resolute, principled, persistent, objective, independent, and impartial in the implementation of my mandate, which I continued to fulfil in a constructive manner. Eventually, things began to take a turn for the better, and the support of the international community and of the civil society organisations in Cambodia never wavered.

The overwhelming support for my work – particularly from the youth, human rights defenders, and friends in Cambodia – encouraged me the most. Thanks to the efforts of those fighting for human rights, including myself, the leader of the opposition was able to return to the country to participate in the political process following a royal pardon;[11] a number of leading human rights defenders were released from prison; and the government returned to a normal mode

9 Letter to the author from Sam Rainsy, president, Cambodia National Rescue Party (6 August 2014) (on file with the author).

10 Letter to the author from Sam Rainsy, President, Cambodia National Rescue Party (9 June 2014) (on file with the author).

11 Royal Decree NS/RKT/0713/827, 12 July 2013 (Cambodia).

of cooperation with my mandate. After a year of protesting against alleged electoral irregularities, opposition party members joined the National Assembly and the government accepted the rationale for electoral reform contained in my reports. Accordingly, on 1 October 2014, the National Assembly passed a bill turning the National Election Committee into a constitutional body, thereby implementing one of my long-standing, key recommendations.[12]

Regarding judicial reform, three long-overdue fundamental laws were enacted in the autumn of 2014: the Law on the Status of Judges and Prosecutors; the Law on the Organisation and Functioning of the Courts; and the Law on the Organisation and Functioning of the Supreme Council of Magistracy. Although these laws are by no means perfect, I believe that they provide a framework for improvement in the future. Therefore, I welcomed the enactment of these laws, but pointed out the lack of adequate consultation with civil society and the lack of transparency in the process of their enactment.

Two prominent political prisoners – including Mam Sonando, the director of a radio station that was critical of the government – were released from jail upon my advocating for them, and others were accorded better treatment. During my second mission to Cambodia, I visited two journalists, Mr Hang Chakra and Mr Ros Sokhet, who were imprisoned in Central Correctional Centre 1, on the outskirts of Phnom Penh, on charges of defamation. When I met the minister for the interior afterwards, I urged him to explore how the two journalists could be released, arguing that in a democracy, they would not have been imprisoned for criticising the policies of the government or of government ministers. Three months later, Hang Chakra was released from prison after being pardoned by the king to mark the Khmer New Year.[13] The day on which I completed my second mission to the country, his sister published a letter in the country's main national daily newspaper, *The Cambodia Daily*, entitled 'UN Envoy should be praised for helping imprisoned journalist'.[14] I welcomed

12 Hul Reaksmey, 'Lawmakers Enshrine Election Panel in Constitution', *Cambodia Daily*, 2 October 2014.

13 Letter to the author from Mam Sonando (on file with the author); letter to the author from Sam Rainsy, president, Cambodia National Rescue Party (on file with the author); letter to the author from the editor of a main national daily English newspaper (on file with the author).

14 Ros Rada, 'UN Envoy Should Be Praised for Helping Imprisoned Journalist', *Cambodia Daily*, 29 January 2010, at 12.

this public acknowledgement of the positive outcome of my prison visit, and hence I ended my mission in Cambodia on a positive note.

My Approach to Implementing the UN Mandate

Many people both within and outside the UN have asked me about the lessons to be drawn from my experience as the longest-serving special rapporteur for Cambodia. Therefore, I would like to outline my experience and the approach that I adopted in discharging my mandate.

First, I took a constructive approach. In other words, I did not seek to name and shame, but rather to listen and offer suggestions to address harmful practices. My mandate was to assist the government in managing the transition to a more democratic society, not to point fingers. Discussing the shortcomings of their system of governance with a UN official is challenging for any leader of a sovereign country. I maintained a focus on harmful practices and injustices, and offered constructive remedial recommendations. I did not take aim at individuals, but endeavoured to keep everyone engaged in the dialogue.

Second, I carried out thorough fact-finding missions in Cambodia, to ensure that my work was informed by accurate information. I also wrote my reports myself.

Third, as an international lawyer, I took a professional approach to the human rights problems in Cambodia. I was principled and ethical in my approach, which earned me the respect of people across the board. I maintained my objectivity, impartiality, and independence throughout my tenure, which required me to be an international diplomat, a human rights activist, a human rights law academic and a government adviser all at once.

Fourth, utilising the flexibility of the UN mandate, I defined the objectives of my mandate and practices employed, which I implemented in the manner I thought would be most effective.

Fifth, rather than regarding myself solely as a human rights envoy focused narrowly on the thematic, technical, and mechanical aspects of human rights, I assumed the role of a political envoy as and when I deemed it desirable to do so, expanding the scope of my work and taking into account the totality of the political situation which had a direct bearing on human rights in the country. Politics and human rights are, of course, intertwined.

Sixth, I selected those areas for closer examination for which I thought I was most suited in terms of my expertise and background. I knew that the institution of the special rapporteur was a weak mechanism, but it was a mechanism which could show direction. Therefore, I chose the areas which I thought needed the most attention and at the same time those in which my engagement could effect change.

Seventh, when making my case to reform the state institutions that were responsible for upholding people's rights, I relied on a comparative analysis that I had conducted in a number of other developing countries with better and stronger democracies, such as the Philippines, India, South Africa, Ghana, and Brazil. I deliberately did not draw comparisons with the British, French, or US systems. Furthermore, I drew on the personal experience I had previously gathered when working on the Royal Commission on Judicial Reform back in Nepal – a country similar in many respects to Cambodia.

Eighth, I sought to engage the government and keep the lines of communication open. I maintained my diplomatic decorum and professionalism when subjected to unfair criticism, harassment, and intimidation by the government in an effort to silence me. Professor Pen Ngoeun, an adviser to the government and one of many vocal critics of my work in Cambodia, posted an article on the website of the Council of Ministers commenting on my determination to stay in the country and my persistence in having my recommendations implemented. He wrote: 'A consummate diplomat, [he] will not leave acrimony behind nor stain his swan song'.[15] He added that I had a 'thick enough skin to withstand the attacks from all sides. Facing untenable situations many UN officials … washed their hands and walked away – right or wrong who cares? Not Prof. Surya Subedi'.

Ninth, I established and maintained formal and informal diplomatic and political channels with the people in government to convey my concerns and to request information. On some occasions, I wrote directly to the prime minister, who responded to my letters.

Tenth, I was sensitive to the Asian notion of 'losing face'. I did my utmost to be respectful to the people in government and tried not to put them in an awkward position in public. I was more candid in delivering

15 Pen Ngoeun, 'UN Special Rapporteur Surya P. Subedi, His Moment to Take Final Credit on His Job, His Swan Song to Cambodians', *Agence Kampuchea Presse*, 16 January 2015, www.akp.gov.kh/?p=56883.

my message to the prime minister in person and maintained a balance so as not to deviate from diplomatic decorum in public. I was aware that every nation has its own pride and I deeply respected the pride of Cambodia, with its rich, ancient Hindu–Buddhist cultural heritage.

Eleventh, I gave credit to the people in the government where it was due, which encouraged individuals to remain engaged with me. Any acknowledgement of a positive contribution to my work could be used by these individuals for publicity, often in amplified form, aimed at the domestic audience.

Twelfth, I always remained optimistic, even in adversity, and kept my hopes alive for a constructive dialogue between the government and the opposition party that would result in beneficial changes.

Thirteenth, I built a personal rapport with several key people in different walks of life in Cambodia, including the leaders of the opposition party, members of civil society organisations, and the media. By doing so, I made it harder for the government to dismiss my recommendations or my services.

Fourteenth, I forged alliances with the foreign diplomatic community in Phnom Penh, who stood by me in difficult times. They offered one more way to engage with the Cambodian government. The Japanese ambassadors, for example, often acted as an intermediary between me and the government.

Fifteenth, I chose soft diplomatic language to deliver difficult messages to the government. In one of my reports, I said that the Cambodian judiciary was not independent in the most diplomatic manner. Commenting on the style of my reports, *The Phnom Penh Post*, which is an independent and critical English daily newspaper in Cambodia, observed:

> At first sight, the report [my report to the UN] may appear to give a positive outlook for the human rights situation in the country. But if you read in between the lines, you will find one of the most powerful indictments of the Cambodian Government in years.[16]

Sixteenth, I understood from the very beginning that the UN is an organisation with its own imperfections and that the UN human rights

16 Nicolas Agostini, 'Overcoming Cambodia Fatigue', *Phnom Penh Post*, 30 September 2014, www.phnompenhpost.com/overcoming-cambodia-fatigue.

section was chronically underfunded and understaffed. Therefore, I was one of those few UN special rapporteurs who never complained about any shortcomings in the level of support provided by the UN in discharging our responsibilities. I accepted the fact that once you volunteer for such a position, you must commit your private time to do the job to the best of your ability and mobilise all other resources at your disposal. Consequently, the UN staff and many assistants in Geneva and Phnom Penh provided me with a superb level of support throughout my mandate, which enabled me to perform my duties well.

Seventeenth, I maintained a balance by taking a principled and pragmatic stand on various issues, and I believe that this approach helped me greatly.

Eighteenth, I was driven by my desire to make a tangible positive impact on the situation of human rights in Cambodia, and I maintained this focus throughout my mandate. Other matters became secondary. My objective was not to score points against a government, but to make a difference to people's rights in the country.

Nineteenth, while maintaining a dialogue with senior members in the government, I also remained in close connection with the opposition party. Sam Rainsy, the leader of the opposition party, visited me in England several times during his exile in France for confidential conversations about his views and concerns.

Twentieth, I became a rallying point for human rights NGOs and other human rights defenders, all united in our collective endeavour. I built a personal rapport with leading human rights activists, who became crucial allies in my dealings with the government.

Twenty-first, I was always mindful of the fact that, as an independent special rapporteur, you have to handle any fallout from your reports yourself. The UN has no mechanism to come to your rescue if governments become hostile. That was the fate of my predecessor and I came close to it myself. The argument for non-action heard in the corridors of the UN buildings in Geneva is that if the UN intervenes in defence of a special rapporteur, then its impartiality could be questioned. The implication of this is that special rapporteurs should be left to their own devices.

Twenty-second, I made every effort to keep ambassadors from key countries informed so that they knew what was going on and supported me when needed. After all, they were the decision makers within the UN Human Rights Council. I knew that I would come under sharp criticism from the government of Cambodia after releasing a report stating that the National Election Committee was not independent and that sweeping electoral reforms were necessary, and that I would need the backing of key countries for my work. Consequently, they stood by me when I needed their support. As anticipated, the Cambodian government turned hostile towards me after the release of the report. I was on the verge of being declared *persona non grata* in Cambodia. Had this happened, I would have been unable to continue working with the government or to have my recommendations implemented. My reports would have been left on the shelves gathering dust, like so many UN reports.

The Cambodia mandate turned out to be more challenging and demanding than I had anticipated. It was a very sensitive brief and I often felt like I was walking a tightrope. I enjoyed the challenges and tried to strike a balance in my approach, fully aware that I had to maintain my impartiality, objectivity, and independence in my work. The appointment was a privilege and a source of intellectual as well as personal satisfaction.

Securing a Place in Heaven

During my six years in the volunteer role as the UN special rapporteur, I did my best to stand up for and protect the human rights of the people of Cambodia, where many such issues were tied to land rights. Prime real estate was being land grabbed by major companies for lucrative developments, while poorer residential communities were being evicted in the process. I found human rights work to be demanding, taxing and emotionally draining, and motivated by care. I spent most weekends and British holidays, as well as all my free time during the week, fighting these harmful practices, which left poorer communities in tatters, and supporting those individuals who led resistance campaigns, some of them in prison. I received a high volume of emails from Cambodia most days of the year, to which I responded swiftly to reassure people and provide the support they sought. When I left the position, a great many Cambodians – including the elderly, women, and the voiceless – thanked me for my work and blessed me. Dharma, karma, and the transmigration of souls are part of the Hindu–Buddhist heritage in both Nepal and Cambodia, so I hoped that my service in

Cambodia would suffice to have earned salvation – moxya – a place in heaven when I finally depart this world.

I was deeply moved by a sketch published in *The Times* newspaper of London[17] after Nelson Mandela had passed away. It depicted him ascending directly to heaven and ordering the pearly gates to open rather than waiting for Judgement Day to decide whether he should be allowed in. Mandela had done so much good in the world that he held the authority and power to release the gates to heaven for himself, and as he approached, they opened to welcome him in. I was inspired by this sketch, so much so that it became a source of spiritual strength during the highs and lows of my time in Cambodia.

The Bhagvad Gita has been guiding me all my life. During my work in Cambodia, I found the following verse to be particularly helpful: 'Anger leads to clouding of judgment, which results in bewilderment of the memory. When the memory is bewildered, the intellect gets destroyed; and when the intellect is destroyed, one is ruined'.[18] I always carried a pocket-size copy of the Bhagvad Gita during my visits to the country and referred to its wisdom for guidance when encountering adversity. When I was humiliated, harassed, and intimidated by the Cambodian government, I stayed on my course, never responded in anger, but dignified and unswervingly focused on stopping the harm that was being done to so many groups of people in the country.

Ripples from the Impact of my Mandate

Aware of my struggles and achievements for the people of Cambodia, a group of prominent international law professors and ambassadors from different backgrounds who had been following my UN work, as well as the leader of the opposition in the country, and the foreign minister of Nepal, informed me that they had submitted my name for the Nobel Peace Prize. They said they had nominated me for my leadership in ushering in a stronger democracy, genuine rule of law and greater protection of human rights in Cambodia; in averting political violence in the country; and in advancing the process of democratisation in Asia in general and in Nepal in particular.

17 *The Times* (London), 6 December 2013, p 27.
18 Chapter 2, Verse 63 of the Bhagvad Gita.

I felt elated by the nomination and delighted that the leader of Cambodia's opposition, Sam Rainsy, was part of it. I had come to know him as a principled and seasoned politician, an honourable man, and a true democrat. When I was sent a copy of the nomination submitted to the Norwegian Nobel Committee, I was moved by the length and detail of the description of my lifetime's contribution to human rights, democracy, and the rule of law in Nepal and Asia in general, and in Cambodia in particular.

My formal role in Cambodia ended after six years, but since then my ties with the country have remained strong. For instance, the Cambodian ambassador to the UN in Geneva, whose job was to defend his government in the UN Human Rights Council, subsequently came to see me in Leeds, asking whether I would be willing to be his supervisor if he enrolled on the PhD programme at my university. 'You were my opponent on the UN Human Rights Council in Geneva', I said. 'Why do you want me to be your PhD supervisor?' He replied:

> Although it was my job to defend my Government in the UN, I was deeply impressed and inspired by the manner in which you discharged your responsibilities both in Cambodia and in Geneva. I learned a lot from you, I am deeply impressed by your intellectual prowess and would be grateful if you would accept me as your PhD student.

I did indeed accept his request and agreed to supervise his PhD research at the University of Leeds. He performed well and duly obtained his PhD. He himself was quite an impressive man and determined to excel. In successfully completing his PhD, he spent a considerable amount of time conducting research in the UN library in Geneva, while continuing in his position as Cambodia's ambassador to the UN. I enjoyed his regular visits from Geneva for his PhD supervision meetings in Leeds.

Another reverberation from my former UN role came in the form of an invitation to join a discussion panel on the human rights situation in Cambodia on the occasion of the screening of *A Cambodian Spring* in 2018 in the UK. In this documentary-style film, film-maker Christopher Kelly movingly captures momentous events in the fight for human rights in Cambodia during 2013 and 2014 – events that I described earlier in this chapter. The movie was shot during my time in the country as the UN human rights envoy and follows three

Cambodian activists – two mothers and a Buddhist monk – who fight to protect their homes from a giant corporation about to evict their entire community. I came to know the Buddhist monk featured in the film, Venerable Sovath, personally during my time in Cambodia and was delighted to meet him again at the screening of the film in the UK. The film was praised as a 'Gripping Human Drama' by *The Guardian*, as 'Fascinating' by *Time Out* and as 'Remarkable' by *The Independent.* The screening was a great success, thanks to the outstanding quality of the film and the engaging panel discussion that followed with Christopher Kelly and the Venerable Sovath.

5 Contribution to Democracy and Human Rights in Nepal

Political Upheavals in Nepal

In the early 1990s, a British journalist jested that if democracy could succeed in Nepal, it could succeed anywhere – a scepticism that was ultimately well founded. Nepal has experienced manifold tragedies, political upheavals, and insurgencies since it emerged from its centuries-old self-imposed isolation under various oligarchical rules in the 1950s. Nepal has embarked on the road to democracy several times, but the attempts to institutionalise democracy in the country have been shaky at best.

The tumultuous political events in Nepal have affected me personally and have engaged my interest as a lawyer and an academic throughout my life, starting out in my youth as a human rights activist in Kathmandu. With a population of about 35 million and bordering Asia's giants China and India, Nepal has suffered untold political turmoil in recent years, due to poverty, bad governance, and corruption. Nepal has served as a sort of political laboratory, in which all kinds of political systems and ideologies have been tried and tested. Over the years, it has witnessed the adoption and cancellation of several constitutions; a referendum to decide the future political structure of the country; several parliamentary elections; a brutal Maoist insurgency; a royal massacre; a people's uprising; a comprehensive peace agreement to bring the Maoists into mainstream politics; the involvement of the UN to monitor the implementation of the peace agreement; the abolition of the monarchy; and two elections for a Constituent Assembly to write a new constitution based on a republican system of governance, federalism, democracy, inclusiveness, and secularism. Nepal is also a country in which the people have elected Communist parties to power through largely free and fair elections.

DOI: 10.4324/9781003271543-5

Nepal's venerable monarchy was eventually abolished in a peaceful manner through a parliamentary vote, and the last king left the Royal Palace in a dignified manner in 2008, holding a press conference to say goodbye to the throne. Nepal thus changed from a monarchy to a republic and from a unitary state to a federal state, and adopted a mixed electoral system of 'first past the post' and proportional representation to elect its national parliament. These are breathtaking events by any standards and have been truly fascinating for me.

Nepal's Journey to Democracy

Nepal is an ancient state that has existed in various forms for more than 2,500 years. It was the only Hindu kingdom in the world until 2008, when it became a secular state. It was ruled for centuries by a long line of kings from the Shah dynasty, followed by the oligarchical Rana family. When the colonial flag flew over the rest of South Asia, Nepal maintained its independence, which was formally recognised by the British through the 1923 peace and friendship treaty. Until modern times, Nepal was governed on the basis of royal edicts based on the tenets of Hinduism and ancient religious codes such as the Manusmriti and Kautilya's Arthasastra, which sought to regulate both affairs of statecraft and relations between individuals. As Nepal was never colonised by any foreign power and the oligarchical Rana family kept the country in isolation for nearly 100 years, very little direct foreign influence was exerted on the governance of the country until recently. In the 1930s and 1940s, a home-grown movement for democracy took root in Nepal. The Indian independence movement also had a measure of influence on the governance of Nepal. Consequently, in 1948, Nepal promulgated its first constitutional instrument, known as the Government of Nepal Act. It was enacted in the final years of the Rana family rule, when Padma Shamsher was prime minister. However, the Ranas were unwilling to implement a genuine programme of reform. When the people's movement for democracy grew in strength and the Rana rule was overthrown, the Interim Government of Nepal Act 1951 (known as the Interim Constitution) was promulgated, introducing elements of democracy to the country.

The stated objective was to hold elections for a Constituent Assembly to write a new democratic constitution. But this did not happen and the Interim Constitution remained in operation until

1959, when a new Parliamentary Constitution was promulgated by King Mahendra. This democratic constitution, too, was withdrawn by the king when he took over power from the elected parliament and the cabinet led by B.P. Koirala. After considering several different options, King Mahendra enacted a new constitution, known as the Panchayat Constitution, making him the executive monarch and imposing a ban on political parties. This constitution lasted for nearly 30 years and was repealed when another people's movement for democracy in 1990 resulted in the adoption of a new democratic constitution based on a constitutional monarchy, which replaced the executive monarchy.

While the new democratic system was still in its infancy, the Maoists challenged it. They walked out of parliament and began an armed struggle in 1996 to overthrow the monarchy and the parliamentary system of government. At the end of the second phase of the people's movement, the Maoists agreed to work within a democratic framework by signing a comprehensive peace agreement with other major political parties. The Spring Revolution of April 2006 not only ended the ten-year 'civil war' waged by the Maoists of Nepal, but also shook the very foundations of the country's traditional power structure, including the institution of the monarchy.

The promulgation of the Interim Constitution in 2007 officially stripped the king of all of his powers and formally ended the Maoist War; while the third amendment to the Interim Constitution declared that Nepal would be a republic and suspended the institution of the monarchy. After witnessing years of violence waged by Maoists under the auspices of a 'people's war' – which resulted in more than 17,000 deaths, the disappearance of between 1,000 and 5,000 people, and the displacement of about 100,000 others – the guns finally fell silent in 2006. Thanks to a comprehensive peace agreement concluded in November 2006, Nepal was back on the road to democracy. Under the peace deal, the Maoists locked away their weapons under the watchful eyes of the UN and confined their fighters to UN-monitored sites dubbed 'cantonments'.

The main objective of the comprehensive agreement between the Maoists and other political parties was to hold fresh elections to a Constituent Assembly that would draft a federal, democratic, and republican constitution for the country. The purpose of a new constitution was to restructure the system of governance within the country and allow equal access to power to people of all ethnic, religious, and racial groups. The aim was also to empower the traditionally marginalised and oppressed ethnic groups in this highly stratified traditional society, and to eliminate discrimination against them.

My Contribution to Political Reconciliation in Nepal

Although I left Nepal in 1993, Nepal never left me. I continued to contribute to improving political stability, economic development, democracy, and human rights in the country in various capacities from abroad, and made frequent visits back home. 'He lives and works here [in the UK] but Surya Subedi is playing a vital role in protecting his native Nepal',[1] wrote British journalist Sheena Hastings in a feature article about my work entitled 'Mountains Still to Climb as Land of the Himalayas Looks to Future', published in a British newspaper in 2008. I had returned to Nepal after completing my DPhil in Oxford, but it had soon become clear to me that I would be unable to pursue my intellectual interests while holding down a government job in Nepal in uncertain times. The civil service had become heavily politicised following the political changes of 1990 and consequently one was expected to align oneself with a political party, which I was not willing to do.

I went to see King Birendra to obtain advice, and he said that he would understand if I were to return to Europe for a while to gain some worldly experience until the political turmoil had settled in Nepal. He advised me to maintain my political independence and asked me to keep in touch and to continue to advise him on legal matters from Europe. I gladly agreed, resigned from my job in the Ministry of Law and Justice in Nepal and returned to Europe to pursue my academic interests. Throughout the 1990s, the king continued to seek my opinion on all sorts of issues – whether the Mahakali River Treaty or the Tanakpur Agreement with India, or other constitutional matters – and I continued to research and publish on a wide range of legal issues pertaining to Nepal's international relations.

I visited Nepal every year and had an audience with King Birendra each time. Likewise, when the king visited London for medical

1 Sheena Hastings, 'Mountains Still to Climb as Land of the Himalayas Looks to Future', *The Yorkshire Post*, 5 November 2008.

check-ups or other matters, we would meet to discuss issues of national significance. The king also asked me to research new ways to increase the prosperity of Nepal. I explored the possibility of developing Nepal as a financial service centre, similar to Switzerland and other smaller countries. King Birendra supported this venture and sent my report to the government of the day for consideration. However, the project was never pursued by the government, as the politicians seemed preoccupied with looking after their personal and party-political interests.

King Birendra had relinquished his powers as an executive monarch during the political changes of 1990 and had reconciled with his role as a constitutional monarch. Although he came under pressure from various quarters within Nepal to reassert power, he told me repeatedly that he would not do so. Rather, King Birendra was devoted to establishing democracy in Nepal. When he was killed in a palace massacre in 2001, I was devastated.

In the aftermath of the massacre, King Gyanendra succeeded to the throne and he too sought my opinion on several issues of national significance. I kept advising him until he assumed the executive power in 2005, thereby effectively changing his status from a constitutional monarch to an executive monarch. I had been in Nepal two months previously, and his confidant and aide, Sharad Chandra Shah, had indicated to me that the king was leaning towards assuming the executive power. I asked the king a number of questions regarding his purported scheme: 'Why, how and for how long? What are your objectives? What is your exit strategy? What is your contingency plan?' I received no satisfactory answers and advised against the plan. Two months later, King Gyanendra dismissed the elected government and instated himself as the executive head of the new government, thereby wielding absolute power. After analysing the steps that King Gyanendra had taken and seeing the kind of people he had brought to power – most of whom were yesterday's men, out of touch with the current political reality, such as Kirtinidhi Bista and Tulsi Giri – I lost confidence in him. 'The situation of a constitutional king becoming the Chairman of the Council of Ministers is something unimagined by the Constitution and (hence) contrary to the democratic values',[2] I stated publicly.

2 'Parliament's Supremacy is a Risk-Free and Legitimate Solution: Prof Subedi', *Nepal News*, 24 June 2005, www.neaplnews.com.np/archive/2005/jun/jun23/news12.php.

King Gyanendra's regressive actions were doomed to fail. When Nepal's seven major political parties formed an alliance to oppose the king's proclamation, I advised the king both publicly and privately to enter into a dialogue with them with a view to handing over power to the people's representatives. I urged the king to restyle himself as a democratic king or a constitutional monarch. In a number of articles published in the national and international media – such as *The International Herald Tribune* (now *The International New York Times*), which was the main international newspaper at the time – I advised King Gyanendra to engage in talks with Nepal's political parties and outlined my views on the best way forward for the country.[3] I wrote on 4 June 2005 that:

> The king of Nepal has an opportunity to lead the nation toward egalitarianism, plurality and democracy, thereby prolonging the life of the monarchy rather than accepting whatever history may thrust upon him. He should seize this chance to earn himself a place in history as a progressive reformist rather than simply as a monarch who snatched away the rights of the people.

My article was translated into Nepali and published in Nepal by leading media houses. Many outlets in Nepal published editorials supporting me. For instance, in an article entitled 'Ending democracy isn't the answer: Prof. Subedi', *Nepal News* stated: 'A leading scholar on international law, Prof. Subedi has proposed a roadmap to return to democracy and said ending democracy isn't the answer to the problems facing Nepal'.[4] I was deeply concerned about the ongoing violence in the country and the loss of life of so many people, on both the government and the Maoist sides. In an article for *The Kathmandu Post*,[5] I outlined my views on how best to resolve the ongoing political conflict and presented several options on potential ways forward. Since I regard law as a problem-solving discipline, as a lawyer, I have long favoured evolution and reform over revolution, and my endeavours for the country then reflected this ethos. But my advice offered to the king, both in public and in private, fell on deaf ears.

3 Surya P. Subedi, 'Restoring Democracy', *The International Herald Tribune*, 4 June 2005, www.nytimes.com/2005/06/04/opinion/taming-the-king-of-nepal.html.

4 'Ending Democracy Isn't the Answer: Prof. Subedi', *Nepal News*, 24 June 2005, www.neaplnews.com.np/archive/2005/jun/jun23/news12.php.

5 Surya P. Subedi, 'Resolving Political Crisis', *The Kathmandu Post*, 6 March 2006.

Aware that I was advising King Gyanendra to reach a compromise with the political parties, the leaders of the Seven-Party Alliance got in touch to seek my help in finding ways to resolve the political crisis and restore democracy. I thus found myself at the forefront of the intellectual campaign aimed at introducing a comprehensive peace agreement designed to bring the Maoists into mainstream politics and persuade them to work within a democratic framework.[6] My work was valued by all the major political parties in Nepal. For instance, on 1 May 2006, Sujata Koirala – the head of the international relations department of the main democratic party in Nepal, the Nepali Congress Party – wrote to me on behalf of the party and its president, G.P. Koirala, expressing a 'most sincere appreciation for the unwavering support to and strong solidarity with the People's Movement for the restoration of peace and democracy'.[7]

Meanwhile, several politicians from both within and outside Nepal sought my advice in defining the parameters of the UN Mission in Nepal (UNMIN). The UN's involvement was twofold, consisting of a human rights mission and a political mission. While the human rights mission had a broader mandate and was set up for the long term, the political mission was a short-term, limited, and focused mandate. The human rights mission was established by the OHCHR in 2005 when the royal regime adopted harsh measures to clamp down on political party leaders, human rights workers, and civil society representatives. The political mission was launched by the UN Security Council at the joint invitation of the Maoists and the Nepalese government. The main mandate of UNMIN was as follows:

- To support the peace process.
- To monitor the management of the arms and armies of the Maoists and the government.
- To assist the parties in implementing their agreement on the management of arms and armies through a Joint Monitoring Co-ordination Committee.

6 Surya P. Subedi, 'Post-Conflict Constitutional Settlement in Nepal and the Role of the United Nations', in Morly Frishman and Sam Muller (eds), *The Dynamics of Constitutionalism in the Age of Globalisation* (The Hague: Hague Academic Press, 2010), pp 71–87.

7 The letter from Sujata Koirala, head of the international relations department of the Nepali Congress Party, sent by email on 1 May 2006, is on file with the author.

- To provide support for the conduct of the election of a Constituent Assembly in a free and fair atmosphere.
- To provide technical assistance to the National Election Commission to enhance its capacity to administer a credible Constituent Assembly election.

Just as the people's movement in Nepal was unique in bringing down the royal regime through a peaceful, civilised, and disciplined movement, the peace agreement and the constitutional settlement brokered were also extraordinary. Unlike other peace agreements concluded in other parts of the world, the peace agreement in Nepal was not concluded between two warring or opposing sides, or between a rebel movement and the government as such. Rather, it was brokered between two sides which had organised and led the people's movement together, which was a unique situation. Indeed, Ian Martin, the head of UNMIN, observed that Nepal's peace agreement was not imposed on the parties from a distant military base or by external powers or bodies.[8] Instead, Nepal's peace agreement was negotiated between the principal Nepalese political actors themselves.

The UN was not party to the negotiations. However, the UN representative was invited to sign the peace agreement as a witness. Although sent by the Security Council, the UN political mission came to Nepal to assist with tasks specified by the Maoists and the government of Nepal relating to the implementation of the peace agreement. Like the Belfast Agreement, the Nepal peace agreement was a framework agreement which was implemented in different phases involving the management of arms and armies, and finally the holding of free and fair elections for a Constituent Assembly to achieve a more permanent resolution of the problems raised by the conflict.

My Contribution to the Writing of a New Democratic Constitution

The way forward for Nepal after the Maoists had been brought into the political mainstream was to write a new constitution which

8 A seminar presentation by Mr Martin in New York on 3 March 2007, as reported in *e-Kantipur*, 4 March 2007, www.kantipuronline.com/kolnews.php?nid=102554.

promoted the rule of law, human rights, and a culture of democracy. The establishment of democracy in Nepal had been agreed on several occasions, but it failed time and again because there was little appetite among the ruling elite to embrace this model of governance. This is why the country found itself repeatedly embroiled in political turmoil. Thus, the challenge ahead was to institutionalise democratic norms and values in all aspects of political life, so that the country could move forward towards lasting peace and prosperity.

When Nepal was about to commence the process of drafting its new democratic constitution after the peace agreement had been brokered with the Maoists, I helped the government and other political parties to ensure that the new constitution included the fundamental rights and freedoms of the people, and that secularism was enshrined therein.[9] I advocated for the separation of religion from state power and for the grant of religious freedom in Nepal. My work became a point of reference for those campaigning for a secular state.

Prime Minister G.P. Koirala invited me to come to Nepal to advise him on a framework for the future political architecture of the country. After our meeting in Kathmandu, he asked me to develop the ideas I had shared with him in greater detail and send them to him, which I duly did after returning to London. In the meantime, I was also asked to chair a Constitution Recommendation Committee of the Non-Resident Nepali Association (NRNA) and prepare a blueprint for the future Constitution of Nepal. After extensive consultation with different stakeholders, I submitted our report to the Constituent Assembly outlining the framework for a new constitution. Our proposals were well received by the Constituent Assembly, the government, and other stakeholders. We recommended that the new constitution reflect the following principles, among others:

- A commitment to respect plurality of ideas and to protect multiparty democracy.
- Respect for the rule of law, democracy, and human rights.
- A guarantee of the independence of the judiciary and freedom of the press.
- An affirmation of economic and political freedom.

9 Surya P. Subedi, 'Secularism in Hinduism', *The Kathmandu Post*, 1 June 2006, p 4.

- An affirmation of social justice.
- An affirmation of secularism.
- Respect for international law.
- A guarantee of adult franchise and periodic elections.

We recommended that the constitution enshrine the fundamental rights and freedoms of the people – including all rights guaranteed under the Interim Constitution, the Universal Declaration of Human Rights of 1948, and the 1966 UN Covenants on Civil and Political Rights and on Economic, Social and Cultural Rights, and other rights flowing from other international treaties – and abolish capital punishment.

We also stated that while meritocracy and competition were to be the main criteria for appointments at various levels of government, there ought to be provisions for affirmative action in favour of women, Madhesi, Tharu, Janjati, Adibasi, Dalit, and other traditionally marginalised and disadvantaged groups. These measures should be time-bound or the laws to this effect should have sunset clauses until such point at which women represented at least one-third of the candidates fielded by all national and regional political parties, and traditionally marginalised and disadvantaged groups an additional one-third.

We stated that for democracy to take root in Nepal, internal democracy should be firmly embedded within the party-political structure. To this end, we suggested that the constitution should include a provision requiring all recognised political parties to hold elections to choose their leaders at all levels at five-year intervals. Similarly, all parliamentary candidates of individual parties should be nominated by democratically elected local committees of the political parties in the constituencies concerned or through local voting. The two principal documents – the political blueprint that I submitted to Prime Minister G.P. Koirala and the report of the Constitution Recommendation Committee of the NRNA that I chaired – constituted the early foundations of Nepal's new political order, which focused on human rights, the independence of the judiciary, and the freedom of the press.

Prime Minister Koirala endorsed my blueprint for the future constitution and advised me to publicise my views in order to precipitate a meaningful debate on these proposals. Accordingly, I outlined my 'Framework for the Future Constitution' in an article published in Nepal's main national vernacular newspaper, *Kantipur*, on 25 March 2009. In a further article in the same newspaper, I also revealed that I had been advising the prime minister on constitutional and other matters of state.[10] From 15 to 17 January 2010, at an international conference in Kathmandu,[11] I addressed members of the legislative body, the leaders of all major political parties, and other stakeholders – such as lawyers, civil society representatives, and human rights activists – to explain the rationale behind my reform proposals. The then leader of the Maoist party, Dr Baburam Bhattarai, who later became prime minister, agreed with my proposals and thanked me for presenting a comprehensive framework for the future constitution.

While I was publicly and privately assisting Nepal with the drafting of a new democratic constitution, I thought it beneficial to visit the archives of former US President James Madison – the renowned 'Father of the US Constitution', who is celebrated for his pivotal role in drafting and promoting the US Constitution and the US Bill of Rights. I had read some of *The Federalist Papers*, which he co-wrote, and had found them relevant to the current context in Nepal. My understanding was that when writing and promoting the US Constitution, Madison's central aim was to establish political stability at the heart of the governance, with a clear separation of powers and checks and balances among the three branches of the government, so that the US could become a strong, prosperous, and unified country underpinned by the freedoms and personal liberty of its citizens. This was successfully achieved through the US Constitution and the institution of a powerful, directly elected executive presidency, building strong foundations for the US to become the world's most powerful nation – economically, politically, and militarily. I thought that Nepal could learn from the political thinking of Madison and Thomas Jefferson, and I therefore visited archives in Washington DC that held collections of historical documents pertaining to their work and records of the drafting of the US Constitution. My study tour of these archives even took me to Madison's residence in Montpelier, Virginia, where I attended talks on his contribution to laying the cornerstone of the US Constitution.

10 Surya P. Subedi, 'Mother, Brownlie and Koirala', *Kantipur*, 16 April 2010 (in Nepali).

11 'The Dynamics of Constitution Making in Nepal in the Post-Conflict Scenario', organised by the Nepal Constitution Foundation, Tribhuvan University Faculty of Law and the Supreme Court Bar Association.

When I mentioned the purpose of my visit to Tom Veblen, a friend of mine, he and his wife Linda – long-term residents of DC and well connected among the city's intellectual community – did everything possible to facilitate visits to places of interest. Originally from Minnesota and of Scandinavian origin, Tom is very knowledgeable of Madison's life and his contribution to the drafting of the US Constitution, and I benefited greatly from my conversations with him during my stay in DC. Back in London, I wrote a report on my research into styles of government conducted in the archives in Washington, arguing vigorously in favour of a US-style presidential system in Nepal. I sent a copy of this report to the leaders of all major political parties in Nepal and published a summary of it in *Kantipur*.[12] I also published a series of related articles[13] in *Kantipur* on the future governance of the country, and on 15 September 2014, I published an open letter to all members of the Constituent Assembly, urging them to opt for a presidential system of government in the new constitution.

Presidential versus Parliamentary System of Government

One reason why I decided to champion a US-style, directly elected presidential system of government, rather than retaining the Westminster-style parliamentary system of government, was the political instability that Nepal had suffered throughout the 1990s and early 2000s under the parliamentary system. None of the elected governments survived its full term. Prime minister after prime minister kept dissolving parliament before it could run its full course. Consequently, mid-term elections became the norm, to the detriment of the country. The parliamentary system was also expensive to sustain and politicians had become corrupt. Various people came to power, but none was able to transform the country. They were all embroiled in petty politics to preserve their power base within the parliamentary system of governance. These frequent changes

12 Surya P. Subedi, 'America, Great Britain and Nepal's Constitution', *Kantipur*, 25 January 2012 (in Nepali).

13 Examples include 'Constitutional Way Out of the Current Political Stalemate', published in *Kantipur* on 6 April 2010, arguing in favour of a presidential system of government in Nepal; and 'The Framework for the Future Constitution', published in the same national daily on 25 March 2009.

in government produced a long line of ex-prime ministers within a short period of time – most of whom were still vying for power, even though none had governed the country well while in office.

In a country such as Nepal – which is home to more than 50 political parties, ranging from the ultra-left to the far right on the political spectrum, and some 126 ethnic groups, all claiming their own stake to power – I thought it would be difficult to achieve political stability through a parliamentary system of government. I could foresee a repeat of the political instability, corruption, and constant horse-trading in parliament that characterised the 1990s and early 2000s. The new political architecture of the country had already served to undermine the bedrock of democracy – that is, meritocracy and free and fair competition. I anticipated that the introduction of proportional representation in electing people's representatives, as opposed to a first-past-the-post system, would increase the difficulty of maintaining a stable government.

Over the decades, politics in Nepal had become the preserve of mediocre people who had failed in other walks of life. Consequently, the country was unable to attract the most suitable people to politics. I was confident that a presidential system would encourage talented, visionary people to choose a career in politics and help to lead the country out of poverty and underdevelopment. Once elected for a term of five or seven years, the president would unify the nation and help foster the political stability needed to further Nepal's economic development.

In acknowledgement of my work towards political reconciliation and the protection and promotion of human rights, as well as the roadmap to democracy that I had presented to the nation, I was nominated by the intellectual community as a potential candidate for the presidency of Nepal if the country were to opt for a presidential system of government. For instance, Sarita Poudel highlighted my strengths in an article published in *Kantipur* and explained how Nepal would stand to gain by electing someone like me as president.[14] I was also enthusiastic about the idea if the institution was to be a directly elected executive presidency rather than a ceremonial one, because I appreciated that the parliamentary system in Nepal had failed to provide the

14 Sarita Poudel, 'Bisheshagyanko Upayog (Utilising Expertise)', *Kantipur*, 9 June 2008.

necessary political stability and ease poverty, and was keen to help remedy this situation.

Constant squabbling among the major parties, frequent changes in government, increasingly corrupt political practices, and the absence of the best and brightest from political life had stunted Nepal's political and economic development. I aspired to create the opportunity for a visionary, strategically minded president to lead the country to prosperity. This is why I campaigned for a presidential system of government similar to that of the US, and my arguments were well received by the intellectual community. The main national English daily newspaper, *The Kathmandu Post*, published the following assessment of my campaign in its editorial article:

> Professor Subedi made an impassionate please to Constituent Assembly (CA) members to act prudently when the deliberate and vote for institutional choices on the form and mode of governance for Nepal. According to Prof Subedi ... Nepal needs a transformative constitution that will enable the country to secure fast-paced development. A development-oriented constitution should mean a basic rule of law to herald an era of democratic political resilience and stability.
>
> It is our earnest duty and responsibility, Prof Subedi exhorted the CA members, to create an institutional environment through the constitution that will allow Nepali citizens to participate in open electoral competition to get elected directly to the post of executive prime minister or president. What prompted an academic of international renown ... to make an appeal in favour of a directly elected chief executive is quite understandable.[15]

However, my endeavours also attracted criticism. For example, a former law minister who was opposed to the idea of a presidential system of government alleged in *Kantipur* that I was trying to become the 'Henry Kissinger of Nepal' – which I took as a compliment, given the geopolitical prowess of that esteemed US politician. When Pushpakamal Dahal – aka 'Prachanda', one of the political leaders of Nepal – asked me to campaign for an executive-style presidential system of government, I agreed because I thought this was a good opportunity to promote this model of presidency; however, he mistakenly assumed that I supported his political stance.

I was inspired by the election of towering intellectual figures such as Dr Servapalli Radhakrishnan and Dr Rajendra Prasad as presidents

15 Mukti Rijal, 'Favouring a Chief Executive', *The Kathmandu Post*, 6 October 2014.

of India in the aftermath of the country's independence. Both of these politicians were instrumental in establishing the foundations of democracy and the norms of good governance in India, as well as enhancing the country's profile abroad. I knew that similar positive developments were possible in Nepal. I published an article outlining my approach to promoting democracy and economic growth in Nepal in *Kantipur*, which became a hot topic of conversation in intellectual and political circles at the time.[16] However, I soon realised that Nepal's political leaders lacked the vision and courage to elect someone like me as president and the idea of my candidacy never materialised.

Nevertheless, the new Constitution of Nepal incorporated most of my proposals designed to strengthen the rule of law, human rights, and democracy in the country, which I had suggested in my reports to the government and to the Constituent Assembly. The new constitution is a progressive document that incorporates all civil and political rights, as well as economic, social, and cultural rights of the people. The human rights provisions in the constitution of Nepal are as strong as those in the post-apartheid Constitution of South Africa adopted under the leadership of Nelson Mandela. This was a great source of satisfaction for me.

The Future of Democracy in Nepal

As I am not a political player in Nepal, I have followed the advice given to me by the late King Birendra in 1993 to maintain neutrality and to assist whoever happens to be in power on any given day, as long as they are sincere and committed to raising the Nepalese people out of poverty and strengthening democracy, the rule of law, and human rights. I have thus advised almost all successive governments in Nepal – whether headed by people from the left, the right, or the centre – on a wide range of legal issues. I regard myself as a professional person – a barrister and academic based in the UK – and have upheld my professional ethics and political neutrality throughout.

I have spoken out whenever democracy, the rule of law, and human rights were undermined in Nepal. In nominating me for the role of UN high commissioner for human rights in 2014, then-Prime Minister Sushil Koirala stated that I had provided intellectual support whenever

16 Surya P. Subedi, 'The Political Options of Today', *Kantipur*, 23 June 2010 (in Nepali).

these values came under attack. The Britain-Nepal Academic Council, which I founded and chaired for ten years, was the first intellectual organisation to oppose King Gyanendra's move in 2005 to transform his role from a constitutional monarch to an executive monarch. I urged him both publicly and privately to collaborate with the main political parties in order to return to democracy. Had he heeded this advice, perhaps the monarchy would not have been abolished in 2008; a ceremonial monarchy could have existed to provide political stability at the top level of governance in Nepal.

There is still much work to do in Nepal to strengthen democracy and the rule of law, and to ensure greater respect for human rights. The particular challenges ahead include:

- Ushering the country towards a new era of economic development through political stability.
- Ensuring inclusivity in all aspects of governance.
- Managing identity politics.
- Addressing the concerns of the Madheshi people.
- Decentralising power through the new federal structure.
- Enhancing the independence and capacity of the judiciary.
- Controlling corruption.
- Addressing issues of transitional justice.[17]

These challenges have resulted from the changing political landscape in Nepal. The ways in which they are met must work for all Nepalese people, regardless of social strata.

Unfortunately, the parliamentary system of governance that the new constitution adopted has not led to political stability; indeed, many of my reservations against this system turned out to be well founded. Nepal is too complex a nation – ethnically, racially, and politically – for the parliamentary system to work. In addition, the absence of a strong principal leader in the form of an executive president at the heart of government has made it easier for India to interfere in Nepalese politics; and in recent years, China has followed suit. The country is

17 I outlined my vision in a public lecture on 'Human Rights and Constitutionalism in Nepal' at the London School of Economics and Political Science on 13 February 2019; www.lse.ac.uk/south-asia-centre/assets/documents/LSE-Public-Lecture-Human-Rights-and-Constitutionalism-in-Nepal-13-Feb-2019.pdf.

now being pulled in opposite directions by its two large and powerful neighbours, to the detriment of a strong Nepalese political, cultural, economic identity.

The Hindu Kush area – that is, the Himalayan Belt, extending from Myanmar to Afghanistan, and including parts of Nepal – has long endured external interference and internal political upheavals because of its strategic significance to regional and global politics and long-standing territorial and boundary disputes among the states in the area. During the old Cold War rivalry between NATO and the Warsaw Pact countries, the smaller countries within the Himalayan Belt suffered exponentially. This was one of the reasons why King Birendra proposed in 1973 that Nepal be declared a ZOP. Given the risk of a new Cold War between China and the West, the Hindu Kush area is once again likely to be drawn into the conflict over the expansion of the spheres of influence of both sides. Nepal could thus revive the idea of becoming a designated ZOP for the benefit of the Nepalese people and those of the wider Hindu Kush area. Its proposal for recognition as a designated ZOP was endorsed by 119 different countries in the 1970s and 1980s; but Nepal has failed to leverage this diplomatic capital since 1990. The time has come to revive this idea to safeguard the country from external interference of any kind. The country of Lord Buddha is well placed to serve as a ZOP.

The parliamentary system adopted in Nepal more than 30 years ago has failed to deliver the political stability needed for economic growth; nor has it produced a political figure who can unify the country, lead it towards prosperity and inspire talented people to enter politics. Most of Nepal's political leaders from 1990 to the present day have been unprincipled tacticians, interested only in gaining and remaining in power, rather than visionary leaders who can command the respect of the population and usher the country towards stronger democracy, genuine rule of law, and greater respect for human rights. Nepal's constitution is democratic; however, the culture of governance is not entirely so, as the present-day political leaders have not yet fully embraced democratic norms.

By its very nature, democracy is a messy system of governance, characterised by power sharing, power struggles, and the need to accommodate competing interests. Still, its operation need not be as disappointing as has been the case in Nepal over the past 30 years. Almost none of today's political leaders can speak with authority, intellectual gravitas, and impeccable moral standing, and can recognise the changes that are required to lead the country accordingly.

On these grounds, I still hold the view that countries such as Nepal would be better served by a presidential system of governance which would attract gifted, skilful people with vision and from varied backgrounds to politics, and enable them to lead the nation towards greater political stability and economic prosperity – just as a long line of US presidents have done. Thanks to the presidential system of governance, people such as President Obama have been able to progress from law professor to president, and to lead the nation in an exemplary manner for two full terms. For an optimist like me, the desire to return to public life and bring about tangible change for the Nepalese people remains strong; only time will tell how things develop in the years to come. When I visited Nepal to speak at an international conference organised by the Nepal Branch of the International Law Association in 2014, I was touched by the words of the then president of Nepal, Rt Hon Mr Ram Varan Yadav. Addressing foreign delegates at his inaugural speech, he said: 'I also welcome Professor Subedi – but he is one of ours'. This was met with a round of applause from the conference audience. I believe that this kind of capital – the warmth and support that I enjoy in my homeland – would help me to contribute towards building a stable and prosperous country founded on the values of democracy, the rule of law, human rights, and equitable and sustainable development in Nepal.

As Nelson Mandela said, while poverty persists, there can be no meaningful freedom;[18] and this is also true for Nepal. Although its centuries-old Hindu–Buddhist tradition embodied many early elements of human rights, such as respect for personal liberty, the country could benefit from an examination of the reasons why Western nations have flourished while it remains impoverished. The prosperity of Western nations is underpinned by values and advancements such as competition, fair play, the rule of law, personal liberty, strong protection of property rights, the industrial and scientific revolution, modern medicine, consumer society, the rise of mercantilism, a strong work ethic, the emergence of the middle classes, the Reformation,

18 Nelson Mandela, 'While Poverty Persists, There Is no Freedom', *The Guardian*, 4 November 2006, p 30.

the consolidation of the nation state and maritime expeditions. While not all of these are necessary to ensure the prosperity of a nation in modern times, some – such as competition, fair play, and the rule of law – are as vital today as they have ever been.

It should also be recognised that democracy is no panacea for all ills in society. Legendary British wartime leader Winston Churchill is often quoted as saying in a speech to the House of Commons in 1947, 'no one pretends that democracy is perfect or all-wise. Indeed it has been said that democracy is the worst form of government except all those other forms that have been tried from time to time.' Democracy is a powerful but imperfect mechanism for governance; it is a set of rules for the resolution of conflicts without bloodshed and for the advancement of society. Good democratic governance is predicated on rigorous respect for these rules; but time and again, Nepal's ruling elite has failed to respect them. There has been too much emphasis on elections and too little on the other essential features of democracy. Too much democracy, through excessively frequent elections, is almost as bad as too little. Over the decades, Nepal's elected rulers have tried to use the mechanisms of democracy to erode constraints on their power. This is one reason why some commentators, such as Kaplan,[19] suggest that Western democracy can be a nightmare for developing countries. However, this need not be the case. Nepal already has most of the conditions required for democracy to succeed, and it is thus within the country's power to defy the sceptics who predict that its efforts towards democracy are doomed to failure. Nepalis may be culturally conservative, but they are politically liberal and highly conscious of their rights, as personal liberty runs deep in Nepalese society.

Nepal has already proved that an ultra-leftist Maoist movement can be brought into the political mainstream through dialogue; that a centuries-old monarchy can be abolished without bloodshed; that a home-grown peace process can deliver positive results; and that a progressive democratic constitution can institutionalise the peace process without the involvement of external powers. I take satisfaction in these developments and in my own contribution to them, despite the challenges experienced in doing so. As the chairman of the London-based

19 Robert D. Kaplan, 'For the 3d World, Western Democracy is a Nightmare', *The International Herald Tribune*, 30 December 1995.

Britain-Nepal Academic Council, I was involved in building public opinion against the Maoist violence and in defending democracy and human rights in Nepal. I regularly wrote articles in both national and international media analysing the reasons for political violence in Nepal between 1996 and 2005, and suggesting potential remedies to resolve it. This is why I dedicated myself to assisting the country's political stakeholders in hammering out a deal for the democratic governance of Nepal. Looking back, I am relieved that my beloved homeland has left those dark days behind. Not only the main Maoist party, but also various splinter ultra-leftist and separatist groups have been brought into mainstream politics. The country has a democratic constitution and is on the road towards establishing a stronger democracy, genuine rule of law, and greater respect for human rights. Peaceful transfers of power have become the norm. What is now needed is the political stability that is conducive to economic development, so that the masses can be lifted out of grinding poverty. The constitution is a living document and there is room to improve it. Embracing a US-style executive presidential system could potentially bring about the much needed political stability in Nepal.

Furthering Human Rights Education in Nepal

Throughout my academic career, I have witnessed first-hand the positive impact that an education in human rights, democracy, and the rule of law can have on young minds – as also reflected by the key role played by the youth in struggles for democracy around the globe, most notably during the Arab Spring of the early 2010s. For this reason, I decided in the summer of 2021 to donate my personal library in London – comprising a large number of books on international law and human rights that I had acquired over three decades of learning and teaching in the UK – to the law library of Kathmandu's main university, the Nepal Law Campus of Tribhuvan University, my alma mater. I am hoping that these books will help inspire current and future generations of students and help equip them for their work to protect and promote human rights in Nepal – as I have tried to do throughout my career, starting out in Nepal and continuing from the UK. Moreover, I set up a sizeable endowment so that the library is in a position to continue to expand its collection going forward. The logistics of this venture proved somewhat challenging: shipping from the UK to this distant landlocked country of Nepal was not an option, so the library of books had to be sent by air cargo at considerable personal expense. However, for me, this paled into insignificance when compared to the value that Nepal's future intellectuals and leaders will hopefully reap from accessing this repository of human rights knowledge.

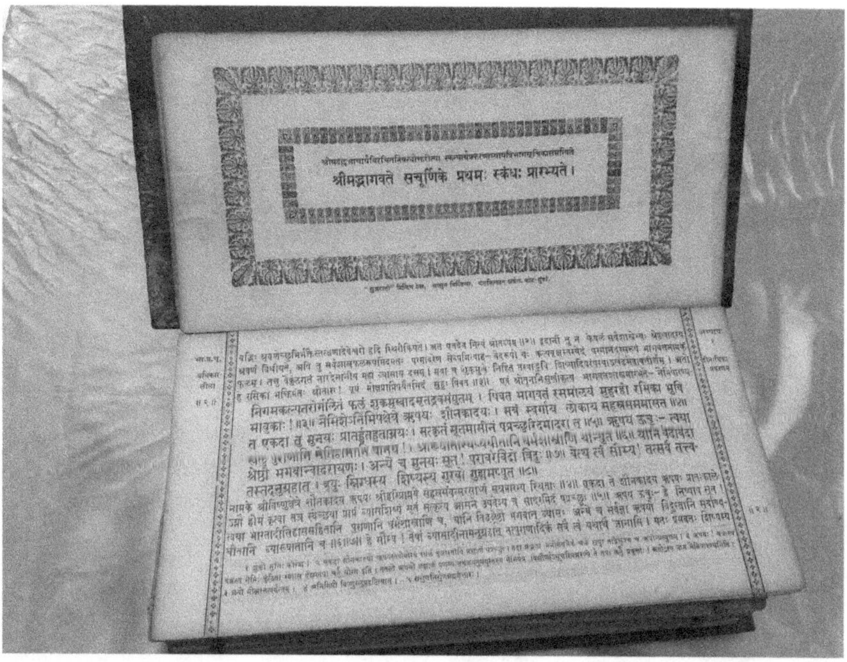

Plate 1 A centuries-old family copy of the Shrimad Bhagavatam at my ancestral home in Nepal

Plate 2 Kathmandu in 1980, speaking as a human rights activist, for which I was arrested the following day

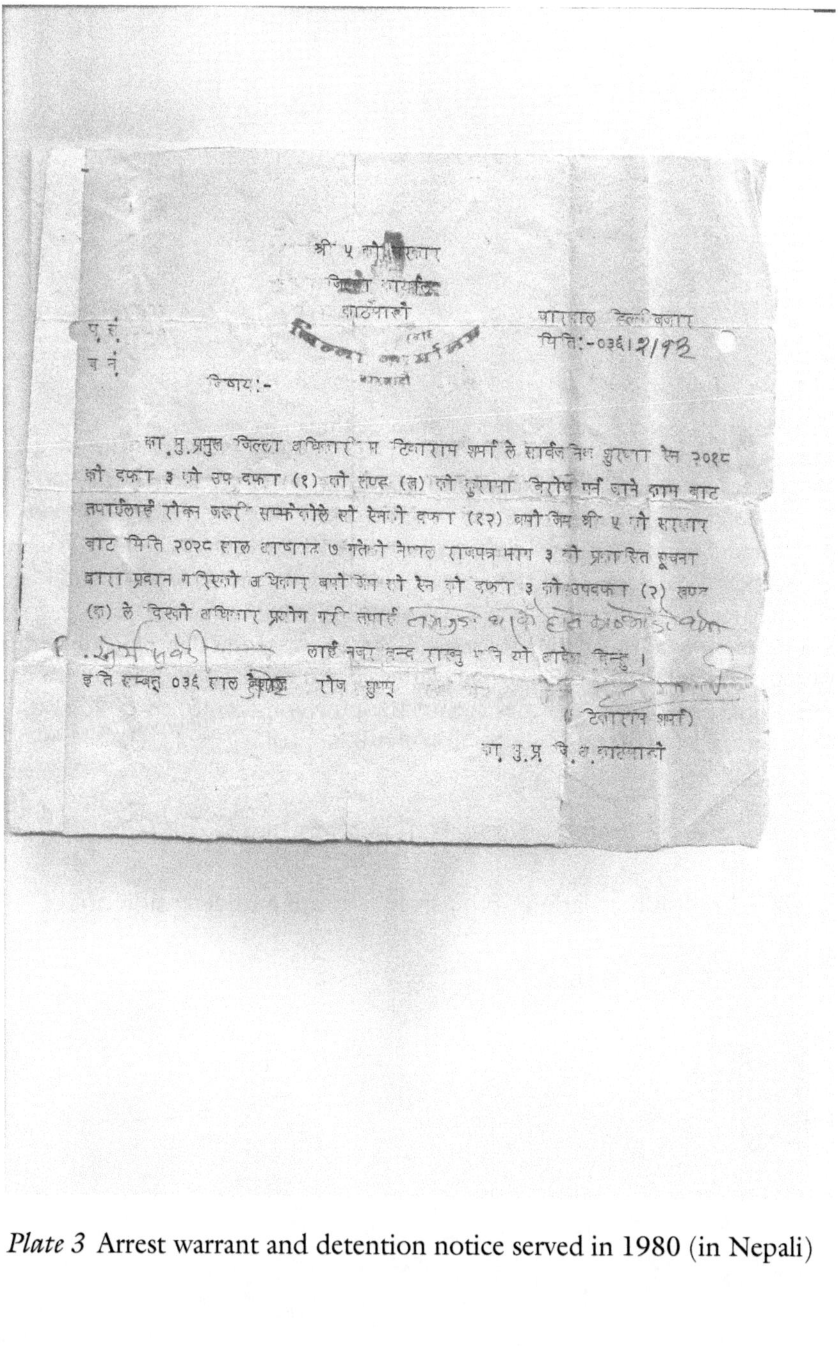

Plate 3 Arrest warrant and detention notice served in 1980 (in Nepali)

His Majesty's Government, District Office, Kathmandu
Chaarkhaal, Dillibazaar
Date: 13-2-2036 (corresponding to 12 May 1980)

I, Tikaram Sharma, Acting Chief District Officer, exercising the powers granted by Section 3, Sub-section 2 (A) of the Public Security Act B.S. 2018 published by His Majesty's Government on 7 Ashad B.S. 2028 in the Nepal Gazette, have felt it necessary to order you, Mr Surya P. Subedi, resident of Kathmandu with a permanent address in Lamjung, to be arrested and detained in order to prevent you from carrying out activities against the provisions contained in Section 3, Sub-section 1 (B) of the Public Security Act B.S. 2018.

(Signed)
Tikaram Sharma
Acting Chief District Officer, Kathmandu

Plate 4 English translation of the arrest warrant and detention notice

Plate 5 Anita after her Law graduation at Oxford, with Pranay

Plate 6 At the OBE investiture with the British foreign secretary and my family in 2004

Plate 7 With Kokila upon becoming a barrister in the Middle Temple in 2007

Plate 8 Delivering an impromptu speech to the media as UN special rapporteur in Phnom Penh in 2011

Plate 9 Speaking to the victims of human rights abuses in Cambodia in 2012

Plate 10 Group photo on the 100-kilometre non-stop walk along the south coast of England to raise funds for Nepal after the 2015 earthquake

Plate 11 At the end of the 96-mile Hadrian Wall Path Walk, dubbed 'Hike the Wall for Nepal', in England with my friend Steve in 2017

Plate 12 At the Palace of Westminster with Kokila and family friend James upon becoming a QC in 2017

Plate 13 Representing a government at the International Court of Justice in 2019

Plate 14 With my family after Pranay's MBA graduation at the Chicago Booth Business School in 2019

Plate 15 Speaking as legal procedural adviser at the IUCN World Conservation Congress in Marseille, France, in 2021

6 My Candidacy for the Position of UN High Commissioner for Human Rights

The Nomination

The position of UN high commissioner for human rights was created with the primary aim of strengthening policy in the areas of international human rights law and humanitarian law in UN member states. It was thus expected that the individual appointed to this position would be from a legal background, with experience and expertise in international human rights law, and would have earned credentials as a professional human rights activist, advocate, or defender. The General Assembly resolution that created the position states that the high commissioner for human rights should be:

> a person of high moral standing and personal integrity and … possess expertise, including in the field of human rights, and the general knowledge and understanding of diverse cultures necessary for impartial, objective, non-selective and effective performance of the duties of the High Commissioner.

Given these criteria, many foreign ambassadors to Cambodia who had witnessed my work as UN special rapporteur encouraged me to consider putting my name forward for appointment as UN high commissioner. Aware of my expertise in human rights, my national and international experience in promoting human rights, and my contribution to democracy, the rule of law, and human rights in Nepal, the leaders of all major political parties in Nepal were likewise enthusiastic in supporting my candidacy for the position.

Encouraged by this support from across the political spectrum, the Nepalese prime minister and the leader of the country's oldest democratic party, Mr Sushil Koirala, officially nominated me in April 2014 to become the next UN high commissioner for human rights.

DOI: 10.4324/9781003271543-6

In his letter to UN Secretary General Ban Ki-moon, the prime minister outlined the contribution that I had made to democracy, human rights, and the rule of law in Nepal. He highlighted the rationale for my nomination in the following words:

> I have the pleasure to inform you that the Government of Nepal has a very senior scholar to nominate for this distinguished position ... Professor Subedi has made an outstanding contribution to human rights at national, regional and international levels and is a person of high calibre with established leadership qualities and proven managerial experience. In recognition of his contribution to the promotion and protection of human rights, he was unanimously elected as the UN Special Rapporteur for Human Rights in Cambodia by the UN Human Rights Council in March 2009. Professor Subedi was assigned to Cambodia with a difficult mandate, but he has performed exceedingly well over the past five years, demonstrating his diplomatic skills, tact and insights required in assisting Cambodia with the process of its political reform and transition.
>
> His constructive engagement with the Government of Cambodia through innovative use of the UN human rights mandate has brought tangible results for the people of Cambodia. I feel that the manner in which he performed during the crisis in Cambodia has elevated him to a 'role model' within and outside of the UN system, human rights community, and especially among the people of the countries fighting for democracy and human rights. He has demonstrated how to win over adversities through a constructive approach: offering positive suggestions to governments while identifying the areas of overall improvement of the human rights situation in the country. The Government of Nepal is confident that Professor Subedi would be able to replicate this success in other parts of the world if he were offered the position of UN High Commissioner for Human Rights.

The prime minister went on to highlight my contribution to the process of democratisation in the country and the intellectual leadership I had provided:

> Professor Subedi has a long and distinguished record of service, including leadership positions in the public, private, and non-profit

> sectors, and continues to advise Nepal on international legal matters and in writing a new constitution. Both the people and the Government of Nepal highly appreciate the contribution that he has made to the cause of democracy, human rights and the rule of law in the country. He was at the forefront of a successful intellectual campaign for democracy in 2005–2006 which ended the rule by an autocratic monarchy and brought the Maoists into mainstream politics, heralding a new dawn for the country. The Government of Nepal, therefore, believes that the eminently qualified Professor Subedi should lead the UN human rights agenda.
>
> Professor Subedi has demonstrated an unquestionable commitment to public service and human rights, whether he is working at national, regional, or global levels. He has the capability to bring valuable insights, innovation and results to the UN OHCHR. He will prove an asset to the United Nations system in general and to the various UN human rights mechanisms in particular.[1]

The prime minister's letter was dispatched to the UN Headquarters in New York, together with a detailed account of my human rights work and my CV. I prepared a document – a kind of manifesto – outlining my case for appointment to this position, with a view to presenting it to the executive team at the UN and the key member states of the UN. This read, in part, as follows:

> I have had direct, recent, relevant and successful experience of work in human rights within the UN system. I know well the UN system of human rights, both from inside and outside, and have a vision for strengthening it. I hold leading positions in several national and international professional bodies and believe that my extensive contacts with professional organizations, academic institutions and international organizations worldwide would enrich the work of the Office of the High Commissioner and enable it to expand its reach.
>
> Given my background and the ethos that underpin my work, I am of the view that I would make an ideal High Commissioner for Human Rights and serve the UN with distinction. I would act

1 A copy of the letter of the prime minister of Nepal to the UN secretary general is on file with the author.

> as a bridge builder between the West and the East and the Global North and the Global South in promoting and protecting human rights under the auspices of the UN. I have had experience of work in human rights for some 30 years at senior level positions in government and academia in both developing and developed countries and in the UN. I have been the UN Special Rapporteur for Human Rights in Cambodia, during which time, by working with the government, I have been able to bring about tangible change in that country. I believe that I meet the requirements for the position and have a unique contribution to make to the promotion and protection of global human rights.

I then spelled out the advantages of appointing a human rights expert to this position, rather than a political heavyweight or diplomat:

> I am of the view that the Vienna Conference on Human Rights of 1993, which led to the creation of this mandate, intended that this senior executive level position within the UN system should be filled by an internationally acknowledged independent expert in human rights with practical experience in a range of areas, including advocacy, advice and publications in human rights, who can command the trust and confidence of the membership of the UN and other stakeholders, including civil society, by his or her own prior experience and expertise in human rights.
>
> Having a human rights thought leader and professional with a proven track record of practical experience, rather than a person primarily from a political, diplomatic or managerial background, appointed to this position would enhance its effectiveness and benefit multiple of stakeholders, including the UN itself. As a person who has been both an insider and outsider of the UN system of human rights and knows well the strengths and challenges of the system, but has not been part of the UN career system, I should be able to bring fresh perspectives to the work of this mandate and be more effective in my dialogue with governments.

I went on to outline what I would do and how I would discharge the responsibilities of the position of the high commissioner:

> If I am appointed to this position, I will make the Office of the High Commissioner a rallying point to promote and protect

> human rights for all and in all countries, paying equal attention to all human rights, civil, political, economic, social and cultural, as well as other rights such as the right to development. I will focus on the protection of the most vulnerable in society and make a special priority to promote and protect women's rights and children's rights, particularly to prevent trafficking and sexual violence.
>
> From my experience as Special Rapporteur for Cambodia, I know that 'naming and shaming' is not the most effective way to affect change. I will offer constructive suggestions to governments and work with them to improve their situation. I will cajole, persuade and argue, with reasons relevant to both the international and domestic contexts, to bring States on board. I will work with Member States to develop realistic and meaningful reforms and win the trust and confidence of all Members to this end. For example, it is vital to develop a system for effective follow-up of the recommendations of the UN special rapporteurs and the resolutions of the Human Rights Council, including the recommendations of the Universal Periodic Review. Utilising my extensive contacts with leading universities and prestigious professional associations, I will develop a mechanism within the Office of the High Commissioner to reach out to such organisations for collaborative study and research and to obtain external funding to support such projects rather than rely on the budget of the UN alone.

Finally, I highlighted the rationale for my appointment as a candidate from Nepal. Born and raised in a traditionally non-aligned country, located between Asia's two giants – China and India – and with no political axe to grind, I embodied an ethos of independence, objectivity, and impartiality. These values have imbued all my activities throughout my life and have enabled me to excel in what I have done.

The Campaign

While in Kathmandu, I was advised by the Foreign Ministry mandarins to meet with as many foreign ambassadors as possible to secure their support for my candidacy. The Indian ambassador, Ranjit Ray, said: 'I had not realised that there was a Nepali as highly qualified as you are. Since there is no Indian candidate, I will write immediately to both the External Affairs Ministry in New Delhi and the Indian ambassador to the UN New York to support you' – which he duly did. The Chinese ambassador said that he had never seen such an impressive CV and promised to write to the Foreign Ministry in Beijing in support of my candidacy.

The Russian ambassador interviewed me for nearly 40 minutes, asking me to explain why Russia should support my candidacy. He concluded from this that I was a well-qualified and deserving candidate, and promised to recommend my nomination to Moscow. The British ambassador likewise reassured me of his support and I later learned that he had written a message of endorsement to the FCO in London. The American ambassador said that he would write to the State Department about my candidacy. The Japanese ambassador – who had consulted Foreign Ministry officials in Tokyo and colleagues in Phnom Penh and New York about my work before meeting me – also confirmed his support; as did the French, EU, Australian, and Swiss ambassadors. After meeting as many ambassadors as possible in Kathmandu, I proceeded to New York to continue to lobby for my candidacy.

In New York, the Nepalese Permanent Mission to the UN organised a series of appointments for me to meet with ambassadors and other key stakeholders, including representatives from the major international human rights organisations. Both the Japanese ambassador and the Indian ambassador asked me to outline why Japan and India respectively should support a Nepali. It was subsequently confirmed that both had met with the UN secretary general to lobby on my behalf. The Swedish and Swiss ambassadors were interested in how I would navigate the financial crisis at the OHCHR and deal with management issues, and confirmed their support after I had explained how I would approach these issues.

The Swiss ambassador was an international lawyer himself and said that he had read some of my publications and had great respect for my work. The US ambassador for the human rights portfolio in the US Permanent Mission to the UN, who was a contemporary of mine at Oxford, suggested that I was the strongest candidate for the position on merit: 'You are just the kind of candidate the UN should appoint'. However, she also indicated that there were some political heavyweights in the ring and that the UN secretary general would have to consider many aspects in making such a high-profile appointment. These remarks sent a chill down my spine. The British ambassador likewise noted that some politically influential candidates had been nominated and admitted that he was unaware of the current thinking of the UN secretary general on this appointment. The Chinese ambassador seemed keen to advocate for my candidacy and sent his deputy to see me again so that I could identify my strongest competitors and explain how my strengths compared to theirs.

Despite this show of support, however, I realised that at the end of the day, the appointment was at the discretion of the UN secretary general. The official endorsement of his decision by the UN General Assembly seemed a matter of formality. The UN secretary general would, of course, consult key members of the UN prior to making his decision; but the power to decide on the appointment was essentially his. Thus, in hindsight, I am not sure whether mobilising ambassadors in Kathmandu, New York, and London to advocate for my candidacy was an effective campaign strategy. At the time, I lacked first-hand insight into how to compete for such a high-level political appointment within the UN. I found the process to be somewhat opaque. Different countries championed their own candidates and lobbied discreetly, without ever expressing support for a particular candidate. As the position of high commissioner is not an elected position, open campaigning was not encouraged. Thus, unless a candidate is already well connected to political figures who are familiar with handling such nominations, it is impossible to know how the process works until one has experienced it oneself. I learned by doing – the hard way.

The Process of Appointment

During the course of my campaign, I realised that the process for appointing the high commissioner was lacking in transparency. No formal selection criteria or timetables were available; and no formal scrutiny of the candidates took place. The secretary general selected the successful candidate in private, with the UN members confirming his decision. The appointment process seemed tightly controlled by the executive team at the UN Headquarters in New York, and resembled more a mission to recruit the CEO of a major international company than a global human rights leader. There appeared to be little in the way of meaningful consultation with member states during the selection process.

Based on this first-hand experience, I am of the view that in future, the following criteria should be applied in order to enhance the transparency, accountability, fairness, and inclusiveness of the process for the selection and appointment of a qualified and effective candidate with appropriate human rights credentials:

- Formal candidate qualifications.
- A record of contribution to the promotion and protection of human rights.
- An official timetable and systematic reporting.
- A procedure for the assessment of candidates.
- A mechanism for meaningful consultation with member states of the UN, both developed and developing.
- Gender and geographic diversity considerations.

In my view, an organisation which advocates transparency, fairness, and democratic principles should practise these values itself. The high commissioner should thus be appointed on merit and through open competition. The procedure for the selection and appointment of candidates should include the publication of an official candidate list at the end of the nomination or application phase; the distribution of candidates' CVs; the submission of statements from candidates explaining how they fulfil the requirements of the position; and panel interviews and Q&A sessions with UN member states and, where possible, key stakeholders such as Amnesty International and Human Rights Watch. However, when I was a candidate for this position, the appointment process lacked such transparency. Candidates were not informed of what the process involved and how it would progress, and it was thus left to us to deduce how things were going through rumours and speculation that trickled down from the Executive Office of the Secretary General in New York. Therefore I concluded that much of my time, effort, and energy in campaigning for my nomination had been futile.

On 8 June 2018, it was announced that a Jordanian prince had been appointed to the position of UN high commissioner for human rights. I was naturally disappointed, but took consolation from the fact that this candidate had spent several years as Jordan's ambassador in New York and was thus already a prominent figure in the UN system. Although a successful diplomat, rather than a human rights expert of international standing, he served well in the role during his appointment.

When I tried to obtain some feedback about my candidacy, I was told that the UN was a political organisation and that politics thus played a major role in appointments to such high-level positions. I had assumed that for the position of UN high commissioner for human rights, expertise and experience in the field of human rights would matter most; after all, this was the intention when the position was created at the Vienna World Conference in 1993. My hopes may have been unrealistic; indeed, I may have been somewhat naïve in setting my sights on this position. Still, I feel honoured by Nepal's nomination and the support I received from so many people. Without competing for the post, I would not have had the chance to learn about the manner of such appointments. This experience will guide me in the future should I be nominated again for an international position.

My Approach to the Role of UN High Commissioner for Human Rights

Had I been appointed, I would have done everything in my power to revamp the UN human rights system to make it more robust and efficient, and better able to meet the challenges of the 21st century. A major shift in the approach to the protection of human rights is required to address the gap between idealism and reality. My proposals included the depoliticisation of various UN human rights mechanisms and the judicialisation of international human rights, to hold governments and individuals in positions of public authority accountable for violations. I would also have worked towards establishing an international human rights court. The UN overall, and many of its human rights bodies, are often seen as political institutions entangled in their own bureaucracy. Consequently, their recommendations are perceived to be moral and political in nature, rather than legally binding obligations.

Additionally, many of the UN human rights bodies lack enforcement powers, and many states thus do not respect their decisions nor implement their recommendations. As these are not binding, the track record of compliance is poor. I am of the view that individuals who suffer from human rights violations should have direct access to an international judicial body – under narrowly defined conditions, so that the international system is not overwhelmed by a flood of cases or frivolous claims. Those conditions could include the exhaustion of domestic remedies prior to resorting to the international mechanism. An international fund could also be established to support aggrieved individuals who are unable to meet the legal costs of this process.

My view is that in the absence of an international judicial mechanism, human rights have been politicised and states often apply double standards in this regard. This has weakened the credibility of the international human rights regime and of UN human rights institutions, and has made it easier for many governments to undermine human rights and the work of UN human rights institutions. The UN treaty bodies are not designed to provide legal remedies against human rights violations, but rather to monitor compliance and suggest correctional measures. Their recommendations are intended to encourage states to take action – for example, by amending existing law and policy, or by introducing new laws and guidance – rather than to provide a remedy for individual victims of human rights violations.

The introduction of legal standards in the field of human rights and the establishment of mechanisms to monitor the implementation of those standards are the primary means through which the human rights objectives of the UN have been pursued. The mechanisms put in place to monitor the implementation of human rights standards include the UN Charter bodies such as the Human Rights Council, the Office of the High Commissioner for Human Rights and the Special Procedures system, as well as several bodies established under various human rights treaties. However, despite their best efforts, these bodies have not been effective in preventing human rights violations and bringing human rights violators to justice. Mechanisms such as the periodic reporting by states of their record in promoting and protecting human rights and the review of such records by various UN human rights bodies should be more robust to increase accountability in this area.

The promotion and protection of human rights have become increasingly complex over the years; yet attempts to reform human rights institutions – whether the system of treaty bodies or the Human Rights Council itself – have barely scratched the surface and have made only marginal differences. In my view, the UN human rights system should be completely overhauled: the UN should move from simply monitoring implementation to actively enforcing human rights. The high commissioner for human rights would be ideally placed to work with UN member states and the secretary general to spearhead these reforms; but expertise in the field is a critical prerequisite for this mission.

7 Extending the Frontiers of Knowledge in Human Rights

Leveraging My Academic Freedom to Promote Human Rights

Ever since my early student days, I have viewed academia as the ideal platform from which to make a contribution to human rights. Brought up in an ethos of universalism and social duty, I had a strong urge to make a difference to people's lives. The knowledge that I gained through my specialisation in international human rights law for my LLM at the University of Hull, and through my research at Oxford into the link between human rights and peace, further whetted my appetite for the subject. I was pleased when I was asked to teach courses on international human rights law on both the undergraduate and postgraduate programmes at Hull, and global governance through law programme at Leeds as well as the master's in international human rights programme at the University of Oxford. These opportunities allowed me to continue to develop my ideas in this field.

British academia has afforded me the freedom to pursue my intellectual interests and an increasingly multicultural British society has made me feel at home in the UK. The mostly indoor lifestyle during much of the year in the rainy British Isles has been conducive to thinking, researching, and writing from the comfort of my study in north London. The hills of Barnet, the meadows of the Dollis Brook valley, and the green belt of Totteridge Common served as pleasant settings not only for recreation and exercise, but also for reflection on contemporary global challenges. Consequently, I have been able to cover the depth and breadth of human rights issues in my publications, from women's property rights to domestic violence, the universality of human rights, the responsibility to tackle land grabbing, to protect land rights, business and human rights, the effectiveness of the UN

DOI: 10.4324/9781003271543-7

human rights system, and a cross-cultural understanding of human rights.

Even when my research and writings focused on other areas of international law, human rights considerations remained at the heart of my thinking. Consequently, a strong human rights theme runs through most of my publications – whether on peace studies, the protection of the environment, the regulation of foreign investment, the expansion of international trade, or the reform of international structures such as the UN human rights system. This chapter summarises those publications which focus on human rights as their primary theme.

My first research project on human rights focused on human rights in public emergencies. I realised that autocratic governments around the globe were using public crises as a smokescreen to curtail human rights. While certain derogations from the human rights regime are permissible in genuine emergencies, in practice such derogations often breach states' obligations under international human rights treaties. Therefore, I sought to analyse the conditions in which such derogations are permissible under international law and published an article on the topic.[1]

This article summed up the rationale, the background, and the main legal principles in international human rights law that govern the right of states to derogate from their legal obligations in emergencies. The article acknowledged that states apply various terms to the special legal order introduced in crisis situations, such as 'state of exception', 'state of emergency', 'state of alarm, 'state of siege', and 'martial law'; but observed that these exceptional situations – which often involve the introduction of special powers of arrest and detention, military tribunals, and limits to the right to freedom of expression, association, and assembly – must be consistent with international human rights treaties, and especially with the 1966 Covenant on Civil and Political Rights. I argued that these treaties provide states with limited exceptional powers designed to restore a constitutional order in which human rights can once again be fully ensured.

Quite early on in my academic career, I also researched the protection of women against domestic violence. My findings were published in an article in the *European Human Rights Law Review*, which

1 Surya P. Subedi, 'Human Rights during Public Emergencies', 3(3) *Obiter Dicta* (Hull University Law Students Journal, England) (1988), pp 25–31.

generated significant debate on the issue.[2] In this article, I highlighted the need for a more robust international legal instrument to protect women against violations of their human rights. I was gratified to see that some of my recommendations, along with those of other actors and stakeholders, were eventually implemented by the UN through the development of new international human rights instruments. Another human rights issue that attracted my attention was the plight of people fleeing wars and civil strife and the protection extended to them under international human rights law, both at home and abroad. My findings on this topic were published in the *Journal of Refugee Studies*.[3]

A different research project focused on the right to self-determination of the Tibetan people.[4] Perhaps due to its geographical proximity to my home country and our shared values and civilisations, I have always been fascinated by Tibet. Often referred to as 'the roof of the world', the country sits on a high plateau sealed off by the Himalayan mountains to the south and east, and by the Qinghai desert to the north. In terms of size, it is almost as big as the European Union. Until 1950, Tibet lived in isolation from the rest of the world under a theocracy led by the Dalai Lama and a hierarchy of monks and aristocrats. As a result, Tibetans rarely registered their independence in international treaties or agreements. This may be one reason why the international community felt no obligation to respond to Tibet's appeal for help when Chinese troops entered the country in 1950.

While the Chinese authorities have always insisted that Tibet is part of China and that matters relating to Tibet are domestic affairs, a considerable weight of authority would challenge these claims, maintaining that Tibet was an independent state until its 'invasion' by China in 1950, and that the Tibetan people have a right to the restoration of independent statehood. Today, however, the international

2 Surya P. Subedi, 'Protection of Women against Domestic Violence: The Response of International Law', 2(6) *European Human Rights Law Review* (1997), pp 587–606.

3 Surya P. Subedi, 'The Legal Competence of the International Community to Create "Safe Havens" in "Zones of Turmoil"', 12(1) *Journal of Refugee Studies* (Oxford University Press, March 1999), pp 23–35.

4 Surya P. Subedi, 'The Right of Self-Determination and Tibetan People', in Dino Kritsiotis (ed), *Self-Determination: Cases of Crisis* (Hull: Hull University Law School, 1994), pp 1–16.

community is more concerned about the human rights situation in Tibet, having recognised the 'one-China' policy with regard to both Tibet and Taiwan. The international community has been reluctant to support the idea of Tibetan independence, due to the principle of sovereignty and territorial integrity of states in international law. The Dalai Lama himself proposed in 1988 that China should handle Tibet's foreign affairs, but that Tibet should have a locally elected government. He also indicated in later years that he was prepared to accept the autonomous status of Tibet similar to Hong Kong.

Since everyone agrees that Tibet is a distinct territorial entity and the Tibetans are a distinct people, Tibetans have a valid claim to the right of 'internal' self-determination. I thus argued that one solution could be to grant real or actual autonomy to the Tibetan people, perhaps along the lines envisaged in the 1951 Seventeen-Point Agreement between China and the Tibetan authorities. 'Autonomy' not only entails the emergence of a new, independent state, but also protection from discrimination and the preservation of cultural, linguistic, and other values. The autonomy that Tibetans are entitled to enjoy under international law should thus enable them to exercise meaningful internal self-determination and control over their own affairs in a manner that is not inconsistent with China's ultimate sovereignty over Tibet.

The Judicialisation of Human Rights and the Reform of the UN System

The UN human rights mechanisms have enjoyed significant success in strengthening human rights, heightening awareness of human rights, and engaging states in a dialogue to promote human rights; but when it comes to holding governments to account for human rights violations, the picture is rather dismal. Unlike in international criminal law or international humanitarian law, where people can be held to account for violations under narrowly defined conditions, in international human rights law there is no provision to hold people responsible for violations. Even when individuals submit petitions to a UN treaty body or to the Human Rights Council, in effect all they can do is to ask states to explain the situation and make recommendations to rectify the law, policy, or situation.

The UN treaty bodies, the Human Rights Council, and the other UN human rights institutions thus cannot bring people to justice for human rights violations, nor can they provide any direct remedies to those whose rights have been violated. In the absence of an international judicial mechanism, human rights have been politicised and states often apply double standards in this regard. This has weakened the credibility of the international human rights regime and UN human rights institutions, and made it easier for many governments to undermine human rights and the work of UN human rights bodies.

This state of affairs troubled me and so I decided to research it in greater depth. My book entitled *The Effectiveness of the UN Human Rights System: Reform and the Judicialisation of Human Rights*[5] casts a critical eye on the rationale and effectiveness of each of the major UN human rights mechanisms, and proposes measures to reform and strengthen the UN system of human rights to ensure that it is sufficiently robust to address the challenges and opportunities of the 21st century. The findings demonstrate that while the global political landscape may have changed in the meantime, the ideology behind the creation of UN human rights mechanisms has not. Today, most of these mechanisms have effectively become paper tigers.

Accordingly, the book argues that the time has come for a major shift in the approach to the protection of human rights to address the gap between the ideal and the reality. Proposals include the de-politicisation of the workings of various UN human rights mechanisms, and the judicialisation of international human rights to hold governments and individuals in positions of public authority to account for human rights violations.

The book highlights the need to establish a direct link between the promises made in the UN human rights instruments and the intended beneficiaries of those promises – that is, individual citizens. The challenge for us today is to chart a path of reform to address the deficiencies of the current rule-based international system and ensure it can evolve in a manner which keeps pace with the political changes taking place around it. The book was well received both by the international intellectual community and by the UN itself, and has contributed to the reform process that is currently underway at this global organisation.

5 Surya P. Subedi, *The Effectiveness of the UN Human Rights System: Reform and the Judicialisation of Human Rights* (Abingdon: Routledge, 2017).

Promoting a Cross-Cultural Understanding of Human Rights

Born into an ancient and unbroken Hindu–Buddhist heritage stretching back some 5,000 years, I was keen to explore whether the scriptures and tenets of these two religions exhibited early elements of human rights. Under both Hinduism and Buddhism – the country's two main religions – the Nepalese people enjoyed considerable personal liberty, including religious freedom. However, they had few political rights. Dissent was allowed only up to a point and political parties were banned. During my youth, the country was ruled by King Birendra as the executive monarch, who was largely a benevolent ruler; but the absence of genuine political rights troubled people like me.

When I went to university to read law, I became a student leader and began to fight actively for political rights. This experience strengthened my resolve to explore whether the two main Eastern civilisations incorporated embryonic concepts of human rights; and whether Hindu and Buddhist tenets were compatible with modern notions of human rights and the rights and freedoms enshrined in the Universal Declaration of Human Rights. I pursued this particular research interest alongside other areas of international law both during and after my academic studies at the Universities of Hull and Oxford.

In 1999, I was invited to deliver a lecture on the concept of human rights in Hinduism at the California Western School of Law. My lecture was published in the *California Western International Law Journal* that same year. Alongside it, the journal editors published a lengthy response to my lecture in the form of an article which they had commissioned from Professor Matthew Ritter. Together, the two articles generated a lively debate in academic circles, which further inspired me to continue my research in this field. My appointment in 2009 as the UN special rapporteur for human rights in Cambodia – another Asian country with a mixed Hindu–Buddhist heritage – also provided new opportunities to study human rights from this particular angle.

I realised at the time that there was an ever-growing fascination with the values of the East – not only in other parts of the world, but also in the East itself – and I was keen to respond to this phenomenon. In the East, people have become increasingly respectful and interested in their own religious heritage, philosophical history, and values, while Eastern concepts such as non-violence, yoga, vegetarianism, nirvana, karma, meditation, and mindfulness have been embraced the world over. Popularised in the West as 'The Light of Asia',[6] the figure of Buddha has long served as a catalyst in generating interest in Buddhism globally. The human rights principles of tolerance, secularism, universalism, and the Middle Way in life have their roots in Eastern civilisations. So too does the international law concept of Panchsheela – the five principles of peaceful coexistence that govern relations among states.[7] These principles were developed over time based on Hindu–Buddhist philosophies – including notions such as 'live and let live', 'the world is one family', and the Buddhist Pañcasīla or Five Virtues, and were enshrined in a trade and cooperation treaty signed by India and China in 1954.

The values of Western civilisations and their contribution to the development of human rights, the rule of law, and democracy have been asserted in a wide body of literature. In contrast, few studies have been conducted on the values of Eastern civilisations and their contribution to the development of human rights in the wider sense of the term. Western scholars are usually unfamiliar with the vast body of scholarship in Eastern civilisations; nor do they go back in history to understand and appreciate the contribution of Eastern civilisations. This intellectual gap renders the work of such scholars limited in scope. There has been a great deal of debate in the recent past about decolonising the curriculum in universities around the globe, and calls have been made for the use of more inclusive and diverse teaching sources.

It was against this backdrop that I wrote a book on human rights in Eastern civilisations.[8] The book explores the cross-fertilisation of values between Eastern and Western civilisations, and how this has taken place. It examines the values of Eastern civilisations and their

6 Edwin Arnold, *The Light of Asia: The Great Renunciation* (London: Kegan Paul, Trench, Trubner & Co. Ltd., 1879). Within ten years of its publication, it had appeared in over 100 editions.

7 The term 'Panchsheela' combines two words in Sanskrit: 'panch' (five) and 'sheela' (virtues). The five principles are as follows:

- Mutual respect for each other's territorial integrity and sovereignty.
- Mutual non-aggression.
- Mutual non-interference in each other's internal affairs.
- Equality and mutual benefit.
- Peaceful coexistence.

8 Surya P. Subedi, *Human Rights in Eastern Civilisations* (Cheltenham: Edward Elgar Publishing, 2021).

contribution to the development of the United Nations' human rights agenda. The study is not limited to human rights in the modern sense of the term – that is, the contemporary notion of human rights that has been developed mainly after the establishment of the United Nations and within the framework of Western political thought. Rather, it considers human rights in a wider sense and within a much longer historical context.

In the book I focus on the norms that underpin Eastern philosophies to assess the extent to which human rights were embedded in the ancient Eastern civilisations. Various chapters examine the expression of values in the scriptures and practices of the Eastern philosophies, tracing their influence on the contemporary understanding of human rights. Rejecting the argument of so-called 'Asian values', which is often used to undermine the universality of human rights, I put forward that secularism, personal liberty, tolerance, and universalism are at the heart of the main scriptures of Eastern civilisations.

My research shows that the values of Hinduism and Buddhism, as derived from the ancient Hindu–Buddhist scriptures, are similar to modern notions of human rights. Secularism in the conduct of a state's domestic affairs, universalism in approaches to the outside world, and adherence to the principle of peaceful coexistence when dealing with foreign powers of different faiths and beliefs are some of the key elements which are deeply rooted in ancient Hindu–Buddhist political thinking. Hindu scriptures composed at the dawn of human civilisation promote the idea of universal fraternity and the equality of all human souls. Peaceful coexistence and tolerance have been at the core of both Hinduism and Buddhism since time immemorial.

Thus, just as today's intolerant religious zealots in India are non-Hindu in character, Communism in China is non-Buddhist, non-Confucianist, and non-Chinese. In fact, Asia's cultural, moral, religious, and philosophical heritage is one of pluralism, universalism, personal liberty, tolerance, secularism, and non-violence in the conduct of domestic affairs, and of Panchsheela in the conduct of foreign affairs.

I further argue in *Human Rights in Eastern Civilisations* that the idea of cultural relativism has been advanced in an attempt to undermine the universality of human rights. Each society is different from others, but this does not mean that the core values of humanity differ from one society to another, from one culture to another or from one religion to another. Admittedly, the nuances of Eastern and Western thought do vary: for example, the former emphasises 'duties', while the latter emphasises 'rights'; the former promotes respect for and coexistence with nature, while the latter seeks to conquer and exploit it for the benefit of humankind; the former affords primacy to family values and spiritual happiness, while the latter champions individualism and materialistic happiness; and whereas the former looks to the ancient scriptures for guidance and meaning, the latter looks to science. These differences in nuances have seen Western societies develop faster than their Eastern counterparts.

However, as *Human Rights in Eastern Civilisations* reveals, some of the core values of 'Western' human rights have strong roots in the Hindu and Buddhist traditions. This shared cultural heritage, integrating Eastern and Western thinking, adds further legitimacy to the universality of human rights and demonstrates how beneficial principles of both Christian and non-Christian traditions can be combined to further the advancement of human civilisation.

The Impact of Unilateral Sanctions on Human Rights

The use of unilateral economic or financial force and other forms of unilateral coercive measures – commonly known as 'sanctions' – has become the preferred foreign policy tool of many states. As a result, the number of sanctions imposed in recent decades has soared, which has significantly affected the lives of citizens in the relevant states. I realised that the imposition of unilateral sanctions, as opposed to UN or collective sanctions, was having a detrimental impact on human rights; but it was unclear what rules were applicable to unilateral sanctions. This troubled me, so I set out to examine the rules governing unilateral sanctions and their interaction with human rights.

In *Right v Might*,[9] celebrated international lawyer Professor Louis Henkin and his co-authors consider whether international law permits the use of military force to promote democracy and human rights. Their book was published in 1989, at the end of a decade of conflict in many countries around the globe. Today, the ostensible use of force to promote democracy and human rights is no longer as common as it was during the Cold War. While the use of armed force as such

9 Louis Henkin et al., *Right v Might: International Law and the Use of Force* (New York: Council on Foreign Relations Press, 1989).

is prohibited under international law and UN sanctions are permitted under the UN Charter, the lawfulness of unilateral sanctions – imposed by one state or a group of states on another state without the authorisation of the UN Security Council – remains a contested issue in international law. Unilateral sanctions have been imposed at will by states – mainly by those with the ability to exert political, military, and economic power – to achieve a variety of objectives, ranging from the pursuit of narrow national political or economic interests to the promotion of the global good, such as the protection of human rights, the prevention of terrorism, and nuclear disarmament.

Unilateral sanctions are supposedly used as an 'emergency button' to address a major impending or ongoing crisis – such as human rights abuses, crimes against humanity, or other internationally wrongful acts by a state – when no alternative measures seem available or adequate to respond to the situation. However, due to the lack of clarity on the rules governing the conditions under which this 'emergency button' can be pushed and the consequences of its improper use, unilateral sanctions mostly operate in a legal vacuum, and differing interpretations of various rules of international law have been invoked to justify both support for and opposition to such sanctions.

Throughout my career, I have advocated for fairness in international affairs, so this ambivalence regarding the lawfulness of unilateral sanctions under international law piqued my interest. In collaboration with a group of scholars from around the globe, I decided to conduct an inquiry into international law as it applies to the use of economic force and unilateral sanctions. I was also concerned by the violations of human rights and of principles of humanitarian law caused by those very same sanctions that were purportedly designed to protect human rights. Therefore, I conceived, designed, and developed a project with a view to publishing a comprehensive treatment of the institution of unilateral sanctions, and invited a number of national and international scholars to contribute to it. The result of this endeavour, *Unilateral Sanctions in International Law*,[10] was published in 2021.

The book investigates the status of unilateral sanctions and the use of economic force and other forms of unilateral coercive measures in

10 Surya P. Subedi, *Unilateral Sanctions in International Law* (Oxford: Hart Publishing, 2021).

international law. It reflects the approach adopted in *Right v Might* in relation to the use of armed force some 30 years ago, as similar issues are presented by the use of unilateral sanctions. The book examines the lawfulness (or otherwise) of unilateral sanctions under international law and the limitations within which they should operate. In doing so, it analyses state practice, the provisions of various international legal instruments on sanctions and the impact of sanctions on other areas of international law, such as freedom of navigation, aviation, and transit; the enjoyment of human rights; the protection of the environment; and the principles of international trade, investment, and regional economic integration.

The book finds that unilateral sanctions, the use of economic force and other forms of unilateral coercive measures – as opposed to 'smart' or targeted sanctions of limited scope – are unlawful unless they meet the procedural and substantive requirements of international law. It identifies and consolidates these requirements, which are scattered across different areas and instruments, and it includes additional rules of customary international law that have emerged from the recent practice of states and have increased the limitations on the use of unilateral sanctions. The book confirms that there is now a positive prohibition in customary international law on the use of economic force if such measures do not meet these requirements. It also concludes that unilateral sanctions that undermine the sovereignty of third states are unlawful under international law.

The book argues that the UN system of human rights does not envisage the application of unilateral sanctions by individual states or groups of states against a target state for alleged human rights violations. Only if neither the UN Security Council nor the Human Rights Council can take or recommend measures can unilateral sanctions be imposed on the delinquent state; and such action must be based on the reports of independent human rights institutions such as the UN special rapporteurs for human rights, independent commissions of enquiry established by the UN Security Council, the Human Rights Council, or the OHCHR. This is because, by violating human rights, the state in question will have committed an internationally wrongful act against all states. The states members of the UN have agreed, both individually and collectively, to protect human rights globally. Thus, any violation of human rights becomes a matter of global concern and an internationally wrongful act against all states, giving rise to state responsibility and the right to take countermeasures or impose sanctions under narrowly defined conditions against the delinquent state.

However, this does not mean that states are entitled to act as judge and jury, decide who has violated human rights, and impose unilateral sanctions on those they find to be at fault. They must follow the norms and procedures stipulated in the UN Charter, human rights treaties, and the resolutions of the UN General Assembly and the Human Rights Council. And importantly, states taking unilateral sanctions are obliged to ensure that those measures do not themselves result in violations of the human rights of citizens in the target state. If sanctions result in the violation of human rights, the state that imposed them will itself have committed an internationally wrongful act, giving rise to its own state responsibility and the right of the target state to take retaliatory countermeasures. Therefore, a balance must be struck between the right of states imposing sanctions and the rights of citizens of target states when invoking the right to protect human rights globally to justify unilateral sanctions.

States have both collective and individual obligations to protect the human rights of everyone, everywhere under the UN Charter, the Universal Declaration of Human Rights of 1948, the World Outcome Document of 2005 of the UN General Assembly and other international human rights instruments. The notion of human rights is recognised as an integral part of international law; thus, the treatment of citizens within a given state by the government of that state is not an exclusively domestic affair, but rather a matter of international regulation and concern. The book concludes that the surrender of certain sovereign rights is therefore an inevitable side effect of UN membership. Membership of the UN involves accepting the exception to the principle of non-interference in the internal affairs of states contained in Article 2(7) of the UN Charter in favour of human rights.

States can discharge their collective and individual obligations to protect human rights by exercising their sovereign rights and taking measures which could fall within the category of 'retorsions' – 'smart' or targeted sanctions of limited scope – against foreign governments, individuals, political leaders, and those associated with power in case of human rights violations. However, any more comprehensive unilateral sanctions would be difficult to justify, because they themselves could result in violations of the human rights of citizens in the target state, and of other substantive and procedural requirements for the imposition of unilateral sanctions. Therefore, decisions to impose more comprehensive unilateral sanctions for human rights violations should be taken only where authorised by the UN or in compliance with the substantive and procedural requirements of international law.

States members of the UN have established various human rights mechanisms and human rights treaty bodies in response to human rights violations. Having established such mechanisms, and having transferred the power to respond to human rights violations to UN treaty bodies, individual states should not undermine these mechanisms and bodies by taking their own actions, including imposing unilateral sanctions on states for alleged human rights violations. If the UN treaty bodies are not effective in protecting human rights, they must be strengthened by further enabling and empowering them. The international rule of law is promoted by strengthening existing mechanisms and the rules governing the conduct of international relations. To this end, the book identifies the rules of international law applicable to unilateral sanctions and proposes measures to implement them.

Reconciling Investment Protection with Human Rights Protection

From early on in my academic career, I have also been concerned about the negative impact of activities of business organisations, and especially of big multinational companies (MNCs), on human rights. I recognised a major deficit in the system for holding MNCs accountable for human rights violations.[11] While MNCs are some of the world's most powerful economic entities, their accountability for human rights violations resulting from their activities worldwide remains unclear and controversial. Although – like all other legal entities – MNCs fall within the purview of the national laws of the countries in which they operate, experience has shown that, due to the complex transboundary nature of their operations, many MNCs can escape their obligations under local law – whether these relate to human rights or the environment. The size, nature, and scope of the activities of certain MNCs give the impression that they are more powerful even than certain smaller states. Their influence is global; their operations are not

11 Surya P. Subedi, 'Multinational Corporations and Human Rights', in Karin Arts and Paschal Miyho (eds), *Responding to the Human Rights Deficit* (The Hague: Kluwer Law International, 2003), pp 171–84.

transparent; they are not accountable to any elected authority; there is no cohesive body of law to regulate their activities; and they also often pursue wealth ruthlessly, at the expense of the environment, human rights, and human values. Therefore many states cannot exercise any effective control over the activities of large MNCs.

Although most MNCs exist to meet a social need, they are driven primarily by the desire for profit. This in itself is no bad thing, as the desire to create wealth has long driven the development of society and has made our world increasingly prosperous. The opportunity to create wealth is important in fostering ingenuity, rewarding invention, and funding the advancement of civilisation. Yet when wealth creation itself undermines its very purpose – to enhance human freedom and human civilisation – observers are entitled to be concerned. One of the overriding concerns among the international community is the responsibility of MNCs to abide by human rights principles in carrying out their activities. Do MNCs have human rights obligations? Should they be held accountable for human rights violations in the countries where they operate?

These questions led me to research the need to reconcile investment protection with human rights protection. MNCs are major vehicles for foreign investment, which has traditionally been regulated primarily by bilateral investment treaties. However, due to the unequal power relations between MNCs and host states, most of these treaties are not designed to address human rights issues. Desperate for foreign investment, developing countries have accepted the conditions of developed countries through such treaties. Hence, it remains unlikely that MNCs as foreign investors will be held accountable for human rights violations in the countries where they invest. Allegations of human rights violations by MNCs range from turning a blind eye to the exploitation of child and women's labour by subsidiaries abroad to paying extremely low wages to local workforces, ignoring health and safety standards at work, and meddling in the affairs of the host state.

However, many governments are either reluctant or unable to impose even minimum international standards on the MNCs that operate within their jurisdiction. It was against this background that I started exploring the need for a more balanced body of law that addresses human rights while protecting foreign investment. I first outlined my proposals in this regard in a paper entitled 'Erosion of State Sovereignty under the Law of Foreign Investment: The Challenge of Balancing Investment Protection with Environmental

Protection', presented at a seminar organised by Mishcon de Reya Solicitors in London in June 2004 and chaired by Professor Judge Sir Christopher Greenwood QC. My ideas were developed further by the Royal Institute of International Affairs in 2005, in a final report entitled 'Following up the World Summit on Sustainable Development Commitments on Corporate Social Responsibility: Options for Action by Governments', prepared by Fanny Calder and Malaika Culverwell under the Sustainable Development Programme of the Royal Institute (Chatham House), London.

The culmination of my work in this field was a book entitled *International Investment Law: Reconciling Policy and Principle*,[12] which was first published in 2008 and has since been translated into Chinese and Farsi by renowned international law professors and published in a number of countries. It is widely regarded as a pioneering work on the need to balance investment protection with environmental and human rights protection, and to interpret the international investment law principle of fair and equitable treatment in a manner that takes account of developments in other areas of international law. Many of the ideas advanced in this book have since been taken up by governments and international organisations in their attempts to reform the investor–state dispute settlement mechanism and strike a balance between different competing principles in developing international investment law. It served as a catalyst for a global debate on the matter, which has resulted in a new trend of including provisions in bilateral and international trade and investment treaties designed to protect human rights, the environment, and other societal values in host states. It is regarded as an authoritative articulation of the state of the law and policy on foreign investment protection and its impact on human rights and environmental protection.

It has been humbling to observe the impact of *International Investment Law* on the development of international investment law. In recommending that the University of Oxford award me the DCL in 2019, the panel of judges assessing my work stated that it had 'undoubtedly contributed to the reform of the sector that is now being seriously addressed by various States'. They further highlighted that I was 'one of the first scholars to analyse the tension that exists

12 Surya P. Subedi, *International Investment Law: Reconciling Policy and Principle* (4th edition) (Oxford: Hart Publishing, 2020).

between protecting the interests of investors and the obligations of States to address other core policy concerns'. Similar complimentary remarks were made by reviewers in leading international law journals such as the *European Journal of International Law* and the *NYU Journal of International Law and Politics.*

Developing the Concept of Zones of Peace in International Law

I have always believed that peace is a precondition to the enjoyment of human rights. Peace, democracy, and human rights are inextricably intertwined. Without peace and human rights, universal values cannot be realised. It is against this background that I began my quest for a possible legal framework for the establishment of both land and maritime ZOPs in various parts of the world. The Cold War, the arms race, and the political turmoil that ensued from the rivalries between the NATO and Warsaw Pact countries were destabilising smaller, weaker states and hindering the enjoyment of human rights in those countries.

During the height of the Cold War, small but strategically located states such as Nepal – sandwiched between the two Asian giants of China and India – felt increasingly insecure. Tibet had been annexed by China in the 1950s and Sikkim by India in the early 1970s. Pakistan also broke up in the early 1970s following the birth of Bangladesh, formerly East Pakistan. These were worrying times for small countries in the region. Nepal was increasingly becoming a target for both US and Russian spies in their efforts to keep an eye on both China and India; and the Indians and the Chinese themselves were deploying their own spies in Nepal to spy on each other. Kathmandu reportedly had the world's largest concentration of spies per capita during the Cold War. These trends would have sent shivers down the spines of the rulers of Nepal. Consequently, King Birendra came up with the idea of establishing Nepal as a ZOP to protect the country from outside interference and possibly even intervention.

The king sought international recognition for his proposal to prevent Nepal from becoming a pawn of not only the two superpowers of the day – the Soviet Union and the United States – but also the regional powers of China and India. His proposal was endorsed by 119 states. At a time when the global arms race was accelerating, the king's proposal resonated not only with other small and strategically located states around the globe, but also with members of the Non-Aligned Movement and states abutting the Indian Ocean, where the arms race had intensified alarmingly. Therefore, during my studies for my DPhil at Oxford, I expanded my research to cover both land and maritime ZOPs in international law. My book based on this research – *Land and Maritime Zones of Peace in International Law*, published in 1996 in the Oxford Monographs in International Law Series[13] – was hailed as an authoritative work not only on land ZOPs, but also on the notion of the use of the seas and oceans for peaceful purposes. It analyses and develops the concept of a ZOP in international law as an instrument to promote disarmament and to protect states' right to peace.

The book examines seven declarations and proposals for ZOPs, relating to the Indian Ocean, the South Atlantic, the South Pacific, the Mediterranean, Southeast Asia, Nepal, and Tibet. Based on the areas they cover and the legal issues they raise, the first four of these are termed 'maritime ZOPs' and the latter three 'land ZOPs'. The book analyses the different methods of creating ZOPs in international law, and assesses the extent to which the principles that underpin traditional concepts such as permanent neutrality and demilitarised zones, as well as similar emerging innovations such as nuclear-free zones and nuclear-weapon-free zones, are applicable to the concept of the ZOP.

Invitation by the UN to Contribute to the Right to Development

As someone who originally hails from a developing country, I have long been intrigued by the notion of the right to development. I wondered what this actually means – is it a right of peoples, states, or individuals? – and how it can be effectively implemented. I was thus glad to accept an invitation by the UN in 2020 to contribute an article about the UN Declaration on the Right to Development of

13 Surya P. Subedi, *Land and Maritime Zones of Peace in International Law* (Oxford: Oxford University Press, 1996).

1986, to its Audio-visual Library in International Law.[14] I sought to bring together different strands of thought within international law to arrive at a concrete meaning of the notion of the right to development, and determine how best to make it a reality. This endeavour led me to write on developmental aspects of WTO law, the law of foreign investment, international watercourses law, international environmental law, the international law of development and development finance, and international economic law.

In an article published in the *Manchester Journal of International Law*,[15] I analysed how, in its early stages of development, international economic law endeavoured to protect the right to property of aliens against the excesses of host states – whether in the form of expropriation, nationalisation, or other forms of interference in the conduct of trade and business. The law was designed to protect the rights of both natural and legal persons doing business abroad. With the establishment of the United Nations, the focus of international economic law instruments shifted to strengthening the economic sovereignty of states, relying on the UN Charter and the right to self-determination of states. This catered to the needs of newly independent states that sought to strengthen their sovereignty and realise the aspirations of their populations. Over the decades, however, that same body of law came to embrace developments that promote and protect the rights of persons and corporate power, to promote economic growth supported by the ideas of free trade and the free flow of investment.

In my view, this change in approach was consistent with the vision of a global order envisaged in the UN Charter, which is founded on the individual pursuit of peace, prosperity, and happiness. At the centre of this paradigm shift are people-centred policies – such as those embodied in bilateral investment treaties, free trade agreements, and WTO agreements – which are designed to empower and benefit both natural and legal persons, including MNCs, rather than state-centred approaches designed to empower governments. This is also true of one of the major areas of international economic law: the law of foreign investment, which has been radically transformed from a body of

14 Surya P. Subedi, 'Declaration on the Right to Development', https://legal.un.org/avl/ha/drd/drd.html.

15 Surya P. Subedi, 'A Shift in Paradigm in International Economic Law: From State-centric Principles to People-centric Policies', 10(3) *Manchester Journal of International Economic Law* (2013), pp 314–35.

law designed to *regulate* foreign investment to a body of law seeking to *protect* foreign investment.

My view is that the economic development of states was one of the central elements of the New International Economic Order and the Charter of Economic Right and Duties of States. This right was reinforced through a 1986 resolution of the UN General Assembly on the right to development.[16] Although the right to development is difficult to define in concrete terms, the articulation of this right in 1986 enabled the international community to rely on it to support and advance other principles of international trade and development, and issues such as preferential treatment for developing countries and the need to address the problem of international debt. It can also be argued that the right to development contributed to the adoption of the Millennium Development Goals by the international community in 2000, at the dawn of the new millennium.

The Declaration on the Right to Development is an ambitious document of programmatic character containing a blend of principles informed by international human rights instruments, together with an aspirational political statement. It introduced to the UN human rights agenda the right of every human being to be able to participate in, contribute to and benefit from economic, social, cultural, and political development. The significance of the right to development lies in the fact that it embodies a comprehensive approach to the realisation of human rights by drawing attention to structures, processes, and outcomes of development, at both the national and international levels.

The Declaration establishes equity, equality, and justice as the primary determinants of development, thereby heralding a new rights-based approach to development. It laid the foundation to advance the UN agenda designed to integrate development into human rights. It has been a catalyst for recognition of the right to development in several subsequent regional and international instruments on human rights and sustainable development. However, the content, nature and status of the Declaration and the right to development itself are contested both by scholars and by states; and the intergovernmental process aimed at reaching a political consensus on its meaning and practical interpretation is highly politicised. Divisions on the

16 Resolution 41/128 of 4 December 1986 of the UN General Assembly.

legal status and implications of the right to development prevail both between and within the Global North and South.

The content of the Declaration is framed along the following main themes:

- A comprehensive approach to development whereby development is defined not solely in terms of economic growth, but as a 'comprehensive' and multifaceted 'process', with social, cultural, political, and economic elements.
- Respect for all human rights and affirmation that human rights are indivisible and interdependent, and that equal attention should be given to economic, social, and cultural rights along with civil and political rights.
- Participation in the formulation of development policies, as the human person is at the centre of development.
- Social justice for all, as the development process should promote social justice, including the 'fair distribution of the benefits' of development and 'equality of opportunity for all' in terms of access to basic resources and services, as well as the eradication of social injustices.
- International cooperation, since the realisation of the right to development requires not only appropriate national policies, but also suitable international conditions for development, with appropriate international policies and cooperation.
- Respect for the right to self-determination, as the Declaration establishes that development 'implies the full realisation of the right of peoples to self-determination'.

The notion of self-determination in this context means that, at a minimum, minorities must enjoy the right to participate in the design and implementation of sustainable development policies.

On the basis of this framework, my contribution to the UN argues that since individuals are the subjects and beneficiaries of the right to development under the 1986 Declaration, they can make claims against the state for the promotion, protection, and fulfilment of the obligations or duties encompassed by that right. As the Declaration promotes 'people-centred development', it makes individuals the beneficiaries of the right to development. The article posits that the 1986 Declaration provides a framework for the adoption of measures to ensure that the development process is respectful of human rights, and of a process through which all human rights and fundamental freedoms can be realised. It firmly places the right to development within the legal framework of international human rights, and links the realisation of this right to international cooperation in the realms of economic development and social justice. It concludes that the concept of the right to development carries with it a moral and political force in the deliberations on economic development of developing countries and the delivery of promises made through various international initiatives, ranging from financing for development and poverty reduction to social engineering projects envisaged in the UN Charter.

Empowering Other Scholars in Human Rights

My passion for human rights and its interface with other areas of international law led to the establishment of a new series of books on 'Human Rights and International Law' by Routledge, a major British publishing house, and my appointment as the editor of the series. The books in this series explore the place of human rights law within the international legal order, offering much-needed interdisciplinary and global perspectives on the increasingly important rule of human rights in the development and implementation of international law and policy.

The series aims to provide critical and contextual accounts of the relationship between human rights and international law theory and practice. To achieve this, volumes in the series focus on major debates in the field, looking at how human rights impact on areas as diverse and divisive as security, terrorism, climate change, refugee law, migration, bioethics, natural resources, and international trade. Exploring the interaction, interrelationship, and potential conflicts between human rights and other branches of international law, books in the series address both historical development and contemporary contexts, before outlining the most urgent questions facing scholars and policymakers today.

The series has afforded human rights scholars from all over the world the opportunity to disseminate their original ideas to a wider audience. Altogether 14 books have been published thus far in this series, extending the frontiers of knowledge in human rights. It has been an honour and a pleasure to work with such first-rate scholars, and has been a source of immense satisfaction. There are numerous intellectual benefits of working as the editor of series and law journals such as this, for instance, the editor gets the chance to read all works submitted prior to publication and can thus keep up to speed on the latest developments in the field. This is especially so with regard to submissions which contain cutting-edge analysis of emerging issues in the area.

Promoting the Rule of Law and Human Rights in Asia

As a vast and populous continent, Asia has seen many human tragedies in modern times. The partition of India in 1947 led to the largest human migration in history, as millions of people moved from India to Pakistan and vice versa. The Vietnam War remains the most dreadful of international conflicts in the post-Second World War period, during which US forces dropped deadly napalm bombs on suspected Viet Cong positions in 1965. In terms of internal wars, the Syrian Civil War, in which Aleppo was destroyed, is one of the most horrendous instances. The Kashmir conflict and the Israeli-Palestinian conflict are among the most protracted conflicts in Asia. The Khmer Rouge regime in Cambodia, the Rohingya crisis in Myanmar and the Saudi Arabia-led intervention in Yemen have also caused terrible human suffering. Campaigns for democracy and human rights of historical proportions in Asia include the Arab Spring of 2011–12, the Tiananmen Square protests of 1989, and the Hong Kong protests of 2019.

Despite being the home of largely peaceful religions such as Buddhism and Hinduism, Asia remains the only continent without a regional or sub-regional human rights treaty, or a human rights mechanism to protect the rights of the people, hold governments to account, and bring perpetrators to justice. Many Asian states – such as Nepal and Cambodia – have ratified most of the core UN human rights treaties, thus subjecting themselves to international scrutiny. However, the special protection enjoyed by the populations of other continents which have committed themselves to regional human rights mechanisms is not available to the people of Asia. ASEAN did establish the ASEAN Intergovernmental Commission on Human Rights in 2009 and adopted the ASEAN Human Rights Declaration in 2012, but this mechanism is very weak.

Notwithstanding the existence of these initiatives, human rights violations are a common occurrence in the ASEAN region. It is feared that the weak Commission may be used as a shield to deflect criticism, rather than a tool to stop human rights abuse in the region. This is because many ASEAN countries were vocal proponents of the 'Asian values' discourse of the 1990s, which promoted Asian exceptionalism to human rights. Many Asian countries with autocratic or semi-autocratic regimes have sought to justify their deviations from international human rights standards by invoking so-called 'Asian values', stating that these differ in some respects from Western values and claiming that international human rights standards reflect merely Western values. These Asian countries advocate a relativist approach. For instance, to justify the Communist Party rule of China, it is often said that the country is developing 'a new system of governance with Chinese characteristics'.

Several questions arise from the tendencies of autocratic governments in Asia to escape their human rights obligations as enshrined in the UN human rights instruments in the name of cultural relativism. What are Eastern values, or Indian values, or Chinese values? Are they different from Western values? How do we infer these values and what is the basis of the claim of so-called 'Asian values', or of a value system with Chinese characteristics? Where do these characteristics come from? Are they the characteristics of the Communist Party of China, or are they based on ancient Chinese history and philosophy?

I recognised the need for a forum for scholars from both Eastern and non-Eastern backgrounds to debate these and many other associated issues, and promote the rule of law, democracy, and human rights in Asia. That is why I played a role in establishing the Asian Society of International Law in 2007, with its head office at the Faculty of Law of the National University of Singapore. Moreover, I became a founding executive editor of its flagship publication, the *Asian Journal of International Law*, upon its launch in 2010. After serving for five years as its executive editor, I was elected chairman of its board of editors in 2015 and I continue to serve in this capacity to this day. This journal, which is published by Cambridge University Press, has provided a platform for debate on contemporary challenges to the rule of law in Asia, among other issues.

Teaching Human Rights in China

In 2015, I was invited to teach a compact course on human rights at one of the main universities in Beijing. In the run-up to my visit to

China, there had been a government crackdown on human rights lawyers and activists, and President Xi Jinpeng had called on Chinese universities to uphold the values of socialism. I was told that there were bound to be government informants and Communist Party members in my class, and some friends in the UK advised me against going to China to teach human rights during the government clampdown. Yet I decided to proceed with the agreed plan: I would be visiting China as an academic rather than an activist, and I intended to teach the course there in the same way as I did in the UK. I thought it was part of my mission in life to spread the values of the rule of law, democracy, and human rights internationally. Thus, my wife and I arrived in Beijing on 8 December, in advance of commencing the course two days later on 10 December – UN Human Rights Day.

Before the course began, I considered exercising caution in what I was going to say in class, as some of my friends had advised. But once I had started teaching and met my students – who were very intelligent, asked probing questions, and participated actively in class discussions – I threw caution to the wind and taught the full standard LLM course in international human rights law in my usual style. We held regular, open class discussions on individual human rights issues in China and elsewhere, examining each in depth and considering all of its aspects. I wondered whether I might be teaching some of China's future leaders in the making.

Emboldened by the fact that nothing untoward had happened to me as yet and that the course was nearly finished, I focused my final lecture on the influence of Buddhist teachings in China when Buddhism was the state religion. Even today, China remains the undisputed home of Buddhism: according to the Pew Research Center, half of the world's Buddhists live in the country.[17] In discussing a potential new system of governance imbued with Chinese characteristics, I thus suggested that this should also incorporate Buddhist values, including personal liberty. I advised that when investigating the origins of their spiritual tenets, the Chinese should return to Confucius and Buddha – which could ultimately lead them to the Rig Veda, the most ancient Vedic

17 '5 Facts about Buddhists Around the World', 5 April 2019, Pew Research Center: www.pewresearch.org/fact-tank/2019/04/05/5-facts-about-buddhists-around-the-world/.

scripture. It is from the Rig Veda that many of the central ideas of Hinduism and Buddhism emanate.

I told my Chinese students that the values of Hinduism and Buddhism, as derived from the ancient Hindu–Buddhist scriptures, are similar to the modern notions of human rights. Secularism in the conduct of the state's domestic affairs, universalism in human approaches to the outside world and adherence to the principle of peaceful coexistence when dealing with foreign powers of different faiths and beliefs are some of the key elements that are deeply rooted in ancient Hindu–Buddhist political thinking. Personal liberty, non-violence, peaceful coexistence, and tolerance have been in the blood of both Hindus and Buddhists since time immemorial. I suggested that by re-embracing Buddhism, China could rediscover its past and honour and contribute to the development of universal values, including human rights. The lecture outlined how Hindu values influenced Buddhist values and how Buddhist values in turn influenced Chinese values, and my analysis went down well with the audience.

During the lecture, I also presented a critical but scholarly analysis of the current human rights situation in China. I worried that the Chinese authorities might not take kindly to this, and that I might be asked to leave the country or to stop teaching human rights. But nothing of the sort happened. Indeed, when the chief editor of the *Chinese Journal of International Law* asked me to contribute to his journal, I said I would be happy to develop my lecture on the human rights situation in China into an article if he would be interested in publishing it. To my surprise and delight, he accepted the article,[18] adding that the publication of critical but balanced analysis was considered acceptable in China.

On the way back to my hotel on the last day of my lecture tour, we travelled by taxi because I had to bring all of my materials and other belongings from the university with me. The taxi driver asked our host, Professor Aifen Xing, where we were from. When she told him that we were originally from Nepal, he told us that he knew some Himalayan songs and would sing them for us as long as we also agreed to sing him a Himalayan song. I agreed and he proceeded to sing

18 Surya P. Subedi, 'China's Approach to Human Rights and the UN Human Rights Agenda', 14(3) *Chinese Journal of International Law* (Oxford University Press, 2015), pp 437–64.

three beautiful Himalayan songs for us. When my turn came, I sang a Nepali-Himalayan song, with the following lyrics: 'My small village is in the lap of the Himalayas, I am the daughter of the Himalayas and my name is "Parbati", or "hill-daughter"'. The taxi driver said he liked my song and the manner in which I sang it; and we all laughed at this delightful and wholly unexpected cultural exchange.

8 The Future of Human Rights

Having strived to promote and protect human rights throughout my lifetime – and having even been imprisoned for the cause – I worry for the future of human rights today, at both the national and international levels. Human rights are guaranteed to all under international law, but sadly this is far from the reality for many people around the globe. The objective is universal, but not the practice. The so-called 'war on terror', the rise of populism, weakened multilateralism, and the resurgence of autocratic governments are undermining efforts to protect human rights globally. I envisage many challenges ahead for the international human rights agenda in general, and for the effectiveness of the mechanisms created to protect human rights in particular. However, I also see the glass as half full, rather than half empty; and I remain optimistic about the future of human rights, for the following reasons.

The Evolutive Nature of Human Rights

The modern concept of human rights – predominantly known as 'civil rights and liberties' until the advent of the United Nations – has evolved over time as an integral part of the rule of law. It has redefined the concept of democracy itself, in the sense that even after winning an election, a government that enjoys the support of a majority – even an overwhelming one – cannot breach the core rights of individuals, including minorities.

In my opinion, embracing human rights has meant embracing modernity, both in the approach to life and in social relations. Human rights are about advancing civilisation – enabling people of any background, origin, race, colour, nationality, creed, and sexual orientation to lead more dignified and sophisticated lives. As societies evolve and

DOI: 10.4324/9781003271543-8

humans become more refined in their lifestyles and thought processes, demand for respect and protection of human rights will continue to increase. The concept of human rights is organic and will keep evolving alongside society through the recognition and addition of new rights, and through new or expanded definitions of existing rights.

Achieving Universality as a Long-Term Project

In my view, the protection of human rights is a long-term objective and the definition of human rights is a never-ending work in progress. The Universal Declaration of Human Rights is not yet a reality in many societies – not only in North Korea and Syria, or the slums of India and Brazil, but also in the inner cities of countries such as the US, the UK, and France, where ethnic minorities, working class populations, and other disadvantaged groups are denied many social and economic rights.

As the notions of the rule of law and human rights are intertwined and evolving, both will survive long into the future – even if the UN or the international legal order in its present form were to disintegrate. Both the rule of law and human rights are now intrinsically associated with human civilisation; and for as long as humans continue to advance their societies, these concepts will remain part of that process – even if they are known by different names in the future. In terms of the development of human rights, our generation is living in exciting times. Huge strides have been made since the establishment of the UN in 1945 towards the creation of a rules-based international society.

Consequently, the international law-making process is regarded as a useful tool in articulating a code of conduct governing relations between states themselves, and between governments and the people within a state. Concerted attempts have been made over the past 75–80 years to introduce international norms and rules of behaviour in many areas of human activity. Currently, there are around 130 separate international human rights instruments (conventions, protocols, declarations, resolutions, codes of conduct, and statements of standards and principles) which form the corpus of international human rights law. These instruments form the basis on which the UN human rights institutions operate and accord a universal character to human rights.

When the heads of state and governments of the world met in New York in 2005 for a World Summit – also known as the Millennium

+5 Summit – they accepted human rights as one of the three central pillars of the UN system (along with peace and security and development). Thus, the debate today is less about whether the human rights values championed by the UN are universal, given that these rights are now regarded as such by all UN member states through the Vienna Declaration of Human Rights of 1993 in general and the 2005 UN Outcome Document in particular. Rather, the debate now concerns the effectiveness (or otherwise) of the mechanisms established to enforce human rights at a global level.

Human Rights in a Changing World

One of the challenges in this regard is due to increased multipolarity in international relations. Much of the international system in general, and the UN human rights system in particular, was conceived in the bipolar world of the Cold War. However, we now live in an increasingly multipolar world, marked by the rise of emerging powers such as the BRICS (Brazil, Russia, India, China, and South Africa), with different political systems and varying degrees of commitment to human rights. Previously, much of the Communist world was on the defensive and was unwilling to stake a claim for leadership in this field on the international stage. Even democratic developing countries such as India and Brazil showed little enthusiasm for the international human rights agenda, inhibited by the questionable human rights situations in their own countries. But this might not necessarily remain the case in the future. As new players ascend to the economic world stage, their populations are likewise demanding their participation in other international forums, including those relating to human rights.

Politically, we have transitioned from the bipolarity of the 20th century through a brief spell of unipolarity in the 1990s to today's multipolar world, marked by the rise of emerging powers such as the BRICS and more recently the MINTs (Mexico, Indonesia, Nigeria, and Turkey). The decline of the Western economic powers – which traditionally wielded predominantly soft power and on rare occasions hard or military power (e.g., the operation in Libya in 2011) to support the UN human rights system – has raised the question of whether that system is fit for the purposes of this new era.

The expectations of the UN human rights system are high; but in practice, the institutions within that system are unable to prevent and address human rights violations effectively. Therefore, I have argued in my scholarly work for the timely reform of the UN system to address the current challenges and prepare for those that lie ahead. This is premised on the idea that even if more fundamental reform of the UN system, such as democratisation of the UN Security Council and the abolition of veto power, is impossible, other reforms which would be more politically acceptable should nonetheless be carried out.

Even if the BRICS do stake their claim to world leadership, they will arguably have no alternative but to retain and reinforce a rule-based system at the international level. Most of the BRICS countries in general, and China in particular, have benefited a great deal from the rules-based system of international trade under the auspices of the WTO, and from the relative political stability afforded by the current international legal order based on the rule of law, democracy, and human rights. They should therefore see the merits of upholding and strengthening this system. Although the UN human rights agenda has its origins in Western political thought, it has now been accepted and embraced by all states worldwide. Even states with questionable human rights records, such as China and Saudi Arabia, do not challenge the UN human rights agenda directly; instead, they plead with the international community to make allowances for their 'national realities' as developing countries that have just started out on the path of political and governance reform.

Thus, even if the economic power of the West continues to decline – and with it, its capacity to champion human rights – those states which seek to project their power internationally and assume global leadership roles – whether BRICS, MINTs, or otherwise – should see the merits of upholding and strengthening the existing rules-based international system, rather than reinventing a new political architecture from scratch. With power comes responsibility. Therefore, whatever might happen to the world politically, the UN (albeit perhaps in a reformed form) and its human rights system are likely to survive for a long time to come.

The Impact of the Rise of China on Human Rights

There are some apprehensions in the democratic world about the possible impact of the economic rise of China on the UN human rights agenda. Concerns have been expressed in certain quarters that this may result in the eventual restructuring of the global political order and institutions in China's favour. A lot has been written about the possible implications of the country's meteoric economic rise for the rest of the world. Since the Bolshevik Revolution in Russia in 1917, Communism has posed several challenges to the international legal order in general, and to human rights in particular.

The Soviet Union and the members of the Warsaw Pact did as much as possible to undermine and neutralise the UN human rights agenda from the inception of the UN in 1945 to the collapse of Communism in Europe in 1989–90. The Soviet Union was one of seven states which did not endorse the Universal Declaration of Human Rights in 1948. Consequently, several compromises had to be reached between democratic states and Communist states during the drafting of many international human rights instruments and the development of the UN human rights machinery. Examples include the conclusion of two international covenants – one on civil and political rights, and another on economic, social, and cultural rights – rather than a single international bill of rights or covenant; and the omission of the right to property – a fundamental human right and a major pillar of democracy and a liberal economic system – from the 1966 Covenants on Civil and Political Rights and on Economic, Social and Cultural Rights. Admittedly, regarding the former, it is also true that two covenants were adopted rather than one due to reluctance on the part of the United States and other Western countries to grant economic, social, and cultural rights the same importance as civil and political rights.

It is somewhat ironic that an international covenant dealing with human rights left out a major economic right – the right to property – from the list of rights that it sought to protect. This could also be one of the reasons why the right to property was not included in the European Convention on Human Rights adopted in 1950. It was only when Protocol I to the Convention was adopted, which entered into force in 1954, that the right to property was recognised.

However, contrary to perceptions in certain quarters that China opposes or will oppose an ideology or political system championed by the West, including the UN human rights agenda, there are no indications that China will in fact do so. As China itself experienced oppressive regimes and foreign subjugation prior to and after the Communist Revolution in 1949, the concept of civil and political rights in the modern sense of the term was alien to China until recently. By contrast, at the height of China's ancient civilisations, the country was home to an advanced and vibrant culture which advocated humanism and the harmony of mankind. The Chinese of the time lived a peaceful and prosperous life, and embraced the teachings of the enlightened Buddha, including tolerance, universalism, personal liberty, and equality. However, in the intervening centuries, Chinese society experienced political oppression; and the basic feature that came to characterise this culture was autocracy, which has little regard for notions of human rights and the protection of human dignity and personal liberty.

Consequently, the core elements of humanism and human rights were lost in China for a long time. Thus, when it comes to democracy, the rule of law, and human rights, China is still in a defensive position. However, the indications are that China will work both with and within the international system: it recognises the benefit of this system, but will try to mould it to suit its own political and economic needs. The only qualification in China's support for the universality of human rights was that when implementing human rights, its 'national realities' should be considered. In its reports to the UN Human Rights Council as part of the Universal Periodic Review, China did not explicitly invoke Communism or socialism to avoid its human rights obligations; rather, it emphasised its status as a developing country with a history of subjugation. China pleaded that it was a developing country whose recent efforts towards economic growth have taken millions of people out of poverty, and that the international community should recognise this achievement. It further claimed that, even if it has not advanced sufficiently in terms of human rights protection and promotion, it was the first country in the world to meet the poverty reduction target set by the UN Millennium Development Goals.

With the rise in China's economic prosperity, there is a rapidly growing middle class which is already seeking increased freedoms; and this demand for human rights and a share in power through democratic means will only intensify in time. The liberalisation of trade and the lifting of barriers to global markets have in turn paved the way for a more liberal approach to government and governance. This is what happened in South Korea and Singapore, and it is likely to happen in China too. China is a member of the UN and joined the capitalist project led by the

WTO in 2001, and it is only a matter of time before the population also clamours to join the 'club' of liberal democracies. WTO membership is not only about economic growth and the expansion of international trade; it is also about increasing and ensuring transparency, accountability and market discipline within the domestic market, and this process must be founded on the principles of the rule of law.

During several academic visits to China, I observed that people were already largely free to live, work, travel, buy, sell, trade, and even worship whatever and wherever they wanted. What was lacking was political freedom. If we believe the ideas advanced by Adam Smith and Amartya Sen, the freedom to conduct economic activities will eventually bring about political freedom too. The Chinese know that the country has flourished not by inventing its own system of economic governance, but by embracing Western capitalism with open arms and jettisoning Marxist economic ideology and Maoist thought. The inner instincts and traits of the Chinese people are not amenable to Communism. This is a system that was imposed on the Chinese people in 1949 and was alien to the masses. But they went along with it because the Chinese Communist Party in general, and its leaders in particular, were regarded as nation builders and restorers of the pride of the Chinese nation.

Today, the younger and increasingly prosperous Chinese population is gradually leaning towards the idea that it is the country's democratic future that will earn and sustain the pride of the Chinese nation. Economic growth alone might not make it possible for China to provide global leadership in the longer term if it does not become a democracy itself. Western civilisation and prosperity were built on human freedom, through which people are free to do as they wish as individuals, provided that they operate within the bounds of behaviour defined and prescribed by the state.

The culture of democracy and human rights has long produced, and continues to produce, self-governing individuals who exhibit a remarkable drive for technological mastery and faith in the utility of economic growth. This has enabled people to be creative and innovative, and to focus single-mindedly on their missions and objectives. Therefore, human rights, individual freedom, and personal liberty are fundamental principles in the West. China (or any ambitious nation) should ultimately realise this virtue and allow its people to enjoy their freedoms in the pursuit of happiness and success.

As a leading member of the UN and a permanent member of the UN Security Council, China cannot escape international scrutiny of alleged human rights violations within the country. This is because – thanks to advances in public international law in general, and in international human rights law in particular – it is now accepted that international restrictions on how governments treat their people do not amount to a violation of the principle of non-interference in the internal affairs of states; and even if they did, they are accepted as a legitimate exception to that principle.

The surrender of certain sovereign rights is an inevitable side effect of UN membership. Membership of the UN involves accepting the exception to the principle of non-interference in the internal affairs of states contained in Article 2(7) of the UN Charter. A logical interpretation of Article 2(7) is that UN interference in the affairs of a state in respect of human rights and fundamental freedoms will not be construed as interference in that state's internal affairs. By deciding to join the UN, a state is accepting the international obligations arising from that membership and thereby the exceptions to the principle of non-interference in internal affairs that may arise accordingly.

The right of other states to express concerns about violations of basic human rights which are of an *erga omnes* character can no longer be included in the definition of 'matters which are essentially within the domestic jurisdiction of any State' in Article 2(7) of the UN Charter. Thus, China cannot legitimately escape international scrutiny of alleged violations of human rights within the country. As a leading member of the UN, China is expected to uphold the principles of the UN Charter, including the protection of human rights everywhere in the world, and to recognise the right of other states to speak out about alleged violations of human rights in the country.

Democracy and the Rule of Law as Global Concepts

Democracy may have its origins in Western political thought, but it is now very much a global concept which has been enriched by similar notions in other civilisations, and by the practices of different states, civilisations, and faiths. There is perhaps no universally accepted definition of 'democracy'; it is a living concept which continues to evolve with time. Today's definition of 'democracy' is underpinned by the core principles of human rights, which was not the case prior to the inception of the modern human rights agenda.

One commentator predicted the end of history in the heady moments of the early 1990s, stating that since the liberal Western political philosophy had triumphed over Communism, the former would remain unopposed; and the world got carried away with this idea.[1] History – let alone democratic history and human ingenuity or innovation – will never 'end'. Human history – and with it the ideas of governance and political organisation of societies – will never cease unless and until the human species itself becomes extinct. Human civilisation, including the pursuit and realisation of democratic values, is an evolving process. Democratic ideals will be further refined and adapted to suit the needs and challenges of any given period, and the world will move on. Similarly, there have been predictions of a clash of civilisations between the Islamic and non-Islamic worlds[2] – an idea which gained momentum in the aftermath of the events of 9/11 at the dawn of the new millennium. Again, there is nothing novel about this concept. Civilisations have clashed throughout human history; people with oppressive tendencies have come into conflict with those with liberated, egalitarian, enlightened, and progressive mindsets; and this will remain the case for a long time to come.

Today, the idea of 'the West versus the rest' propagated by authors such as Samuel Huntington holds little weight. And there are also clashes within Islamic, Christian, Hindu, and Judaic societies themselves, between those with a liberal outlook and values and those with an oppressive mindset. There is little difference between liberally minded individuals in the Islamic world and those with similar attitudes in the Western, Christian, or Hindu world. Therefore, the real clash of civilisations is not, and will not necessarily be, between the Islamic and non-Islamic worlds, but rather between the authoritarian and the liberal; between the autocratic and the democratic; between the conservative and the progressive. Members of both camps can be found in all religions and across all civilisations. There are numerous examples of meetings of liberated minds from different religions,

1 F. Fukuyama, *The End of History and the Last Man* (New York: Free Press, 1992).

2 S. Huntington, *The Clash of Civilizations and the Remaking of World Order* (New York: Simon & Schuster, 1996).

Islamic and non-Islamic, Western and non-Western; and from white, black, and Asian backgrounds.

Where Western values were once racist and imperialist, they have sought to become progressive and liberal. When it comes to human rights, it is becoming increasingly redundant to speak in terms of Western and non-Western values. The concept of the rule of law provided the basis for democratic constitutions around the world and for the international human rights treaties. The current rise of the BRICS countries in general, and China in particular, is likely to diminish the policing role of the West, but not to undermine the essence of the ethos that underpins the UN human rights agenda. Whether Western in origin or not, human rights are here to stay. The real question is not where we came from, but where we go from here. The impetus to continue to promote the value of human rights in principle is secure; but making the protection of human rights a reality for hundreds of millions of people depends on the reform of the UN's human rights system to ensure it can address the challenges of multipolarity.

To conclude, I am of the view that the issues that are currently hindering the protection of human rights around the world are temporary setbacks. The youth of Iran, China, and most Arab countries know their rights and will fight to make their countries democratic, just as I once did myself. The future belongs to the youth, and not to the ageing autocrats who rule them; it is just a matter of time. My experiences of discussing international law and human rights at universities and academic events in the UK and abroad have encouraged me to put my faith in the educated youth. I have seen a spark in the eyes of students from all around the world, and their growing enthusiasm for human rights. When they first arrive at university, students from countries with autocratic or semi-autocratic governments are often eager to defend the status quo out of a sense of patriotism or nationalism. However, as they progress in their study of international law and human rights, they increasingly begin to appreciate the values of liberalism and universalism, and to question the legitimacy and propriety of their autocratic governments. Through teaching international law and human rights, I feel that I have helped to prepare the future leaders of countries big and small, democratic and autocratic, Western and Eastern. In this way, extending the frontiers of knowledge in human rights and expanding access to international human rights literature can have a tangible impact worldwide.

Thus, while the sun may be setting on the West's economic domination of the world, Western values – including democracy, the rule of law, and human rights – will live on (with some local modifications) in the East and elsewhere. The challenge is to reform and revamp existing mechanisms for the promotion and protection of human rights to make them fit for the purposes of the 21st century, and many of my publications are geared towards this objective.

9 Reflections on My Journey

An Appraisal of Life

It has been a long journey, both literally and metaphorically, from a simple village in the foothills of the Nepal Himalayas to the life of a global citizen in Britain. The lessons from my Sanskrit education that one should stretch oneself as far as possible in both gaining and imparting wisdom remain deeply ingrained in me today. In my ongoing quest for knowledge, I have earned almost every qualification and title possible within my chosen discipline – some of which are highly coveted. I have also taught at as many universities as I possibly could around the globe, sometimes holding posts at several universities simultaneously.

Early on in my academic career, I delivered a lecture at the Fletcher School of Law and Diplomacy in Boston, where I had the privilege of spending time with Professor Alfred Rubins, a towering intellectual of his time. As we discussed his extensive body of work – the list of his sole author publications alone runs to some 30 pages – I mused aloud: 'I wonder whether I will ever be able to accomplish as much as you have?' He replied with confidence: 'You will'. Both his achievements and his assurance left a lasting impression on me, and I have endeavoured to follow his example ever since.

Another source of true inspiration was my professor at Oxford, Sir Ian Brownlie – perhaps the most outstanding international lawyer of his generation. He was a generalist who made significant contributions to the development of almost all areas of international law. While I have also attempted to cover the full spectrum of international law during my career, I have latterly come to realise that it was a tall order to try to emulate this range in an age which is characterised by specialism.

DOI: 10.4324/9781003271543-9

My efforts to explore the depth and breadth of international law have admittedly been demanding. I have worked long hours almost every day of my life and have juggled numerous positions of responsibility, both national and international, and both within and outside academia. The life of an academic involves continuous thinking, writing, and researching, 24 hours a day (or at least one's waking hours), 7 days a week, 12 months a year. The distinguished international lawyer Elihu Lauterpacht once said that 'international law is both work and hobby', and I would concur with his assessment.

The following verse from Ecclesiastes rings true for academics – and particularly for international law and human rights academics such as myself:

> For in much wisdom,
> There is much sorrow,
> And who gathers knowledge,
> Gathers pain.

In gaining knowledge, I learned much of people's suffering around the world; and I made it my mission to help alleviate this however I could. This is what kept me going when I was fighting for human rights in Nepal, working for the UN in Cambodia, and advising the British foreign secretary on human rights. In 2014, returning from speaking at the plenary session of the UN Human Rights Council in Geneva, I took a taxi from the airport to my university. As I pondered on the human rights situation in Cambodia, the taxi driver asked me whether I was a professor or the like. I said that I was; to which he responded, 'You are one of the worriers, then'. I agreed with him – most academics worry about the world and try to fix things.

The celebrated British philosopher and educator Bertrand Russell wrote in his autobiography that three passions governed his life: a longing for love, the search for knowledge, and unbearable pity for the suffering of mankind.[1] This resonates strongly with me, and my passion for fairness and justice has guided both my life choices and my work engagements. Whether I have succeeded in my efforts is a different matter; but I have given them my all, and I have been helped

1 Bertrand Russell, *Autobiography* (London: Unwin Paperbacks, 1975), p 9.

by many of those who I have met along the way. I have been fortunate beyond measure to have shared my life with my wife, Kokila, and our two wonderful children, Pranay and Anita. I could never have accomplished what I have without Kokila as my partner. A resilient, fair-minded, and eternally optimistic person, she has worked tirelessly to support me and care for our children.

Much of my human rights work throughout my career – whether advising the British foreign secretary on human rights or serving as UN special rapporteur for human rights in Cambodia – has been voluntary. 'Paid jobs can be more boring. That is why they are better paid', one friend jested. 'Prestigious and stimulating jobs are paid less – and sometimes not at all, if the job is particularly interesting'. Her observation struck a chord with me.

At a diplomatic reception hosted by Foreign Secretary William Hague in 2014 in Lancaster House – a lavishly appointed government hospitality venue located next to Buckingham Palace – my fellow guests asked me about my profession. I replied: 'I am professor of international law at the University of Leeds, an adviser on human rights to the foreign secretary, and the UN special rapporteur for human rights in Cambodia'. One of the ambassadors responded: 'What glamorous positions you have!' Naturally, they knew little of the sacrifices I had made in life to earn them – or that in large part, they were their own reward.

A perhaps less glamorous, but no less valuable, volunteer position came through my association with the Britain-Nepal Medical Trust – a major British medical charity which provides health services to the poor in Nepal. Although I am not a medic myself, I became involved with the trust in 2007 at the invitation of the late Dr Simon Sinclair, a medic friend of mine; and I served progressively as a trustee, deputy chair, and joint co-chair, alongside Dr Gillian Holdsworth. In this role, I travelled frequently to my homeland to assist local teams in reaching out to and helping the needy. When the Nepal earthquake struck in 2015, Dr Holdsworth and I organised and participated in a 100-kilometre non-stop charity walk – dubbed the 'Didi-Daju Dash' ('Sister and Brother Dash') – along the south coast of England to raise funds for the victims. We were joined by a former British ambassador to Nepal, Andrew Sparks, as well as Nicky and Paula Willmore, Rosemary Blandy, and Shona Duncan – long-term supporters of the trust. I followed this up with another fund-raising event in 2017: a week-long charity walk with Dr Steven Turner, Andrew Stuart, and

Andre Tilleman – all long-term Nepalophiles and personal friends and colleagues of mine – along the Hadrian's Wall Path, which stretches from coast to coast in the north of England. During the walk, I wore a top designed and printed by Steven, emblazoned with the words 'Hike the Wall for Nepal' on the front.

Most recently, I was appointed pro bono by the Bureau of the Council of the International Union for Conservation of Nature (IUCN) as legal procedural adviser of the IUCN World Conservation Congress 2021, taking place in the French city of Marseille between 3 and 11 September 2021. Privileged to have the opportunity to assist this prestigious international organisation, I gladly accepted the appointment. Human rights and environmental issues are intertwined; and the degradation of the environment due to climate change, global warming, and rising sea levels presents critical challenges to human survival, human rights, and human dignity – especially for vulnerable communities. A safe, clean, and healthy environment is integral to the enjoyment of many fundamental human rights, including the right to life. International organisations such as the IUCN thus have a significant role to play in safeguarding human rights and human dignity by addressing these environmental challenges.

Overall, the work I have done and the positions I have held, both within and outside my career, have brought me immense satisfaction. When asked to describe my dream job in a speaker profile for an event hosted by an international law association in the UK in 2015, I wrote that my various diverse roles all added up to my dream job: professor of international law at a prestigious British university; UN special rapporteur for human rights in Cambodia; English barrister; adviser to the British foreign secretary; and chief editor of a refereed law journal – the *Asian Journal of International Law*, published by Cambridge University Press. The event organisers read out my answer to the participants and in return I received a round of applause from the aspiring young human rights lawyers in attendance.

The Price of Success

Admittedly, however, success has come at a price – and sometimes a heavy one. As the Nepalese saying goes, what you do when your hair is black will come to haunt you when your hair has turned grey; and this is how I feel sometimes. I have missed out on many of the pleasant mundanities of British life: the conviviality of the pub; the escapism of

TV; the ritual car wash at the weekend; the warm glow of productivity from gardening or DIY. And my children seem to have picked up some of my not-so-helpful habits. For instance, looking at the overgrown grass in our back garden, I asked Pranay one day whether he might mow the lawn, to which he replied that he was busy with exams – and anyway, 'We are a family of thinkers, not lawn mowers'.

At times, I have also felt that my titles have created a gulf between me and my friends and colleagues. Upon my appointment as an OBE in 2004, a mature Indian student said: 'Many congratulations, professor, but many people will now leave you, thinking that you are no longer one of them'. This was echoed in a note received from an old English friend on my appointment to QC: 'Many congratulations, Surya, but now you have left us'.

I often ask myself whether it was necessary to work quite so hard all my life and what impact my work ethic has had on my children. Generally speaking, 'emigrate' and 'energy' go hand in hand, and our home was a veritable intellectual hothouse, with all its pros and cons. Most parents hope that their children will progress further in life than they have done, and I have wondered about the pressure that this expectation puts on their children. Of all the notes I have made in my diaries about my family over the years, two in particular stand out.

The first I made in 1999, when I had just been promoted to professor and was preparing to fly to New York to attend meetings at the UN as a government delegate. We were having a family conversation at the dinner table about our future. I noticed that Anita looked slightly upset, so I asked her: 'How are you feeling, Anita?' She replied: 'Papa, I am worried that I may die without becoming famous – without doing a PhD'.

'I understand', I responded. 'Everyone feels worried at times. But you are just seven years old. People live up to their nineties – or even to 100 these days. Remember what is important to you, apply your strengths and skills to it – even if you feel scared – and you will lead a successful life'.

But Anita was still worried: 'If I die without becoming famous, people might think I was no good'.

Older and wiser, nine-year-old Pranay chimed in: 'Don't worry. Not everyone becomes famous. When you become old, you die. You cannot help it. That is life'.

Anita seemed struck by this bald summary of existence. 'You see? One must become famous!"

'Not necessarily', replied Pranay. 'The main point in life is to become happy. Be happy – that is all'.

The second was a conversation that took place at the parents evening at Anita's school in Hull, Froebel House, in January 2000. The head teacher told us: 'Anita is a wonderful child. I don't see anything lacking in her. She is very bright. You know that, don't you? It has been such a pleasure to teach her. You must be very proud of her. You must be glad that you have such bright children. She is very mature for her age'.

Then she added: 'You yourself have reached the top of your profession, I hear – a professorship?'

I responded: 'Thank you. Yes, for the time being'.

She replied: 'Well, your children have a tough act to follow'.

I still sometimes ponder on this remark to this day. By working hard and progressing as far as I have done, have I inadvertently put unnecessary pressure on my children? In conversation with Anita at home at the dinner table one evening, I was discussing the pastoral care that I provide to my students: 'One student said today that the advice that I had given him was a pearl of wisdom. Do you also think that my advice has been helpful to you?'

Anita replied: 'I am flooded by the pearls and need a break!'

She then asked me what the nicest compliment was that I had received from my students. 'That I was an ocean of wisdom', I replied, to which Anita responded: 'I am drowning in the ocean and need to float away free!'

We both laughed at the same time; but in later years I wondered whether I had been over-prescriptive or pushy, which can be quite typical of Asian parents. This dawning realisation came too late, however, as by then my children were both grown up. I take consolation from the fact that, as a parent, I did everything to the best of my abilities and out of love for my children. The views recently expressed by Prince Harry about his upbringing are a reminder that, even with the best of intentions, parents may not always provide their children with what they really need. On the prince's revelations, one columnist in the *Sunday Times* wrote: 'Parents are always to blame, Harry. Your children will discover that too'.[2] I often wonder what kinds of parents my children will be one day and what kinds of people they will be when they reach my age. I have realised from experience that one must be a parent oneself to appreciate the unconditional love of parents and how much they miss their children once they have left home.

Global Citizen, Global Outlook

Kokila and I brought Pranay and Anita into this world and have done our utmost to give them the best future possible. They are both bright, kind-hearted human beings, and I hope and pray for the best for them. The question I keep asking myself is whether they will be as happy as I have been to live the life of a global citizen. I realise that this may have been easier for me because Nepal never left me, even though I left Nepal. I have always had a social and emotional anchor in Nepal. My worry is that without such an anchor, my children may become free-floating individuals in this vast world, without a sense of belonging to a particular society. Their connection to Nepal is not as strong as I would have wished – I suspect because we did not send them to visit their relations in Nepal during the school holidays every year, as many Asian families in Britain do. Instead, we took them to all corners of the world, encouraging them to explore the globe as confident human beings. Living as first-generation Nepalis in the UK, we had no parents, uncles, aunts, brothers, or sisters from whom to seek advice and guidance on how to bring up our children in the UK.

This feeds into a core issue associated with life as a global citizen: that of national or social identity. At some point in their lives, most first-generation immigrants grapple with questions of cultural identity and belonging. By the same token, their identity is also questioned and scrutinised by the society of their new homeland. As I have spent much of my working life in the UK and have been awarded several British titles, many people and institutions in Nepal regard me as British. Likewise, because I was born and brought up in Nepal, worked for the Nepalese government for several years and continue to help the country in various ways, many Britons regard me as Nepalese. I leave it to others to see me as they wish. I have never challenged

2 Matthew Syed, 'Parents are always to blame, Harry. Your children will discover that too.' *The Sunday Times*, 16 May 2021.

people's perceptions of my cultural identity, as long as I am free to pursue what is important to me. When I was working in Cambodia as the UN special rapporteur for human rights, many people assumed that I was a Buddhist, as I am a native of Buddha's birthplace. I felt no need to correct this, as the core messages of both Hinduism and Buddhism are the same. I also hoped that the assumption would expedite my acceptance into Cambodian society, so that I would be better able to assist in the fight against the country's autocratic rulers.

I stopped worrying a long time ago about how other people see me. I realised that people make up their minds about others based on a limited amount of information which is filtered and perceived through their own unique lens. I have always felt that as long as I am striving to do right in the world, I should not spend any time worrying about other people's perceptions of me.

As much of my work is devoted to promoting human rights, democracy, and the rule of law at an international level, it does not matter where in the world I am physically located. As a law academic, my most abiding loyalty is to the rule of law – whether at the national or international level. As a legal professional with an independent mind, I have been treated as an expert by various governments and international institutions. For example, in 2015 I was appointed as a member of a taskforce by the World Economic Forum, based on my expertise and publications in the relevant field. I was also invited to speak at a high-level meeting on the side-lines of the UN General Assembly in New York in 2017 for the same reason. The colour of my skin and my national background were irrelevant to these and other engagements.

In fact, my global outlook has proved invaluable on such mandates, allowing me to adopt an approach that reflects and recognises the divergent dynamics at play in these often complex scenarios. I have been able to transcend the traditional divide between East and West, developing and developed world, and Global South and Global North in these international fora to arrive at solutions that are acceptable to all sides. For instance, while I was serving as a government delegate to the UN General Assembly meeting in 2001, the Sixth (Legal) Committee sought to adopt an official definition of 'terrorism' in the wake of the 9/11 terrorist attacks in New York and Washington DC. Opinion was starkly divided and reaching agreement on a comprehensive definition looked increasingly difficult. I was therefore tasked with developing a compromise proposal, which was subsequently instrumental in the adoption of the UN resolutions on this subject.

A similar situation arose at the World Conservation Congress of the IUCN in September 2021. Some sensitive and highly charged issues relating to the Global South and Global North were raised during the meetings of the IUCN Steering Committee. Committee members solicited my views, as I had been affectionately dubbed the 'father of the Congress' thanks to my efforts to ensure that the organisation's rules and regulations were respected by all. I outlined my views in an objective, impartial, and independent manner, from the position of an international lawyer rather than a champion of either the Global South or the Global North. The Committee appreciated this input and was thus able to resolve matters in the best interests of the organisation, working towards the higher objective of the conservation of nature and the natural world.

Some Regrets

As the French philosopher Voltaire wrote, 'We all are formed of weaknesses and error: let us pardon reciprocally each other's folly. This is the first law of nature'. We all are amateur humans, one way or another – and I am no exception. I must acknowledge some regrets, both personally and professionally. From a professional perspective, I feel that I have not gathered enough moss at my university, having engaged in so many external activities during my career. The heads of UK law schools often observe that their international law professors 'are everywhere but here'; and I admit that this would apply to me to a certain extent, especially given the time I have dedicated both to the UN human rights system and to diverse causes in Nepal. With regard to the latter, for example, while continuing with my academic research and handling the full complement of courses and PhD supervision at university, I chaired the Constitution Recommendation Committee of the NRNA, which was tasked with preparing a blueprint for a new democratic constitution after the Maoist insurgency had wreaked havoc in the country.

I established the Britain-Nepal Academic Council in London, together with Professor Michael Hutt of SOAS University of London and Professor David Gellner of the University of Oxford, and chaired it for ten years. As previously mentioned, I spent 12 years fulfilling various roles for the Britain-Nepal Medical Trust. I also established the Britain-Nepal Lawyers Association; and I was instrumental in the creation of the NRNA, a global organisation of the Nepalese diaspora which aimed to attract foreign investment – not only financial, but also skills- and knowledge-based – to Nepal. I served for two years as a trustee governor of the National Trust for the Conservation of Nature in Nepal, and I was a member of an expert group that advised on boundary issues between India and Nepal. As a first-generation Nepali living in the UK, the expectation was that I would continue to assist the country and the wider Nepalese community in various respects. These unusual dynamics might not have been so readily understood by my colleagues in the UK. And my children and other second-generation Nepali immigrants would not be subject to the same expectations.

These external commitments left me little time to forge strong bonds with colleagues in Leeds, even though the university has been my main place of work since 2004. The distance between us was exacerbated – both literally and figuratively – by the decision to base my family in London. The focus of my work has also made me something of a lone wolf: while over the years I have participated in some collaborative projects at Leeds – launching new postgraduate programmes, establishing a new research centre for international governance, and organising international conferences – and have supervised many PhD students, much of my research and most of my writing projects have been solitary affairs.

By contrast, in conjunction with peers at both national and international levels, I have established intellectual and academic organisations in the UK and in Asia; worked with international law scholars from around the globe to publish edited volumes on international law; and launched a series of books and a new law journal to enable both emerging and established authors in international law to publish their work. I often feel that I have no natural intellectual home in any specialist area within the field of international law. Due to the broad range of subjects that I have explored during my academic career, I belong everywhere and nowhere, insofar as academic associations and specific interest groups are concerned. Single subject or single issue academics in any specialist area would not regard me as one of them. Instead, both in Nepal and in international legal circles, many regard me as a man of all seasons – a label that I wear with pride.

My regrets in the personal sphere are keener; yet regrets, as the African proverb goes, are much like grandchildren – they come much later in life. No one grows old without gaining a few scars along the way. Regret is natural and a vital part of learning; the key is to avoid sliding into a sense of recrimination and self-judgement. ‘It’s only those who do nothing that make no mistakes, I suppose', the English writer Joseph Conrad surmised. Looking back, I recognise that I may not have always been a model husband or father while I pursued my academic and professional ambitions. That said, I have endeavoured to live as happy a life as I can while I am here on this planet.

Mark Zuckerberg's observation that 'life is about learning from mistakes and figuring out how to move forward' is a reminder that everyone struggles; everyone leads an imperfect life – this is part of the human experience. It is normal to make mistakes and endure challenges in life. When we recognise this is a collective experience, we feel less alone; indeed, we feel connected, part of humankind, and therefore are better able to practise compassion towards ourselves and others. This acceptance helps us to let go and move forward. Writing this memoir has given me the opportunity to relive the precious moments of my life, and to recount the errors made along the way and how I have endeavoured to address them. But writing a memoir does not mean that I am ready to hang up my academic or QC gown just yet.

I have heard many people speak of boredom or burnout, but these words have no place in my vocabulary. Most of my friends and colleagues of my age in Nepal have already retired (the retirement age in Nepal is 58), and most have also become grandparents; likewise, most of my British academic peers have also either retired or switched to part-time employment. However, I intend to continue for as long as I am able, as I thoroughly enjoy my academic work.

Unfulfilled Dreams and the Future

The Mahabharata says that man is plagued with a thousand desires in this world. I do not have that many, but I do have some unfulfilled dreams that I would like to realise one day.

The first is to attend the famous Glastonbury Festival in the UK. I should have done this in my thirties, but I never had the time. Now, none of my family members or friends are willing to accompany me, saying: 'It is not for you'; but I would like to find out for myself.

The second is to visit the moon as a tourist on a commercial flight, hoping that a heavy discount might be offered for an academic, but the odds of that happening during my lifetime are slim.

The third is to launch a new magazine or journal in the UK entitled *The Alternative*, as a forum for people from all backgrounds to express their scholarly views – however radical or bold – as long as they are visionary and constructive, and not contemptuous, libellous, or racist. I have harboured this idea since 1993. Recently, however, a similar publication – *The Journal of Controversial Ideas* – was launched by three professors from the universities of Milan, Oxford, and Princeton.

The fourth is to return to Kathmandu for good, to work on my research and writing projects and to establish a Centre for Himalayan Peace Studies. Although modernity has transformed the city over the past half-century and it now struggles with the impact of pollution and overcrowding, it remains my Shangri-la, and the country traditionally known as the land of meditation and contemplation still offers abundant opportunities to work towards achieving peace both within the region and beyond. The need for such efforts in the Hindu Kush – the Himalayan belt extending from Myanmar to Afghanistan – is as great today as it was when I began my research in peace studies and the notion of a ZOP, during the Cold War. Due to the new rift between China and the West, the region is likely to become an arena for conflict in the future as both sides seek to expand their sphere of influence.

The fifth is to contribute to the establishment of a regional mechanism for the protection of human rights in Asia, as this is the only continent that still lacks such a mechanism. There is a pressing need for this, as most contemporary human rights challenges are to be found in Asia. Given the vast size and incredible diversity of the continent, however, such ambitions may ultimately be impossible to achieve; but if this proves to be the case, at the very least, a sub-regional mechanism for the protection of human rights in South Asia should be established. This idea has been under discussion for some time, and I have enthusiastically supported the endeavours of the OHCHR and other civil society organisations to this effect, and have advised some South Asian governments to work towards it within the framework of the South Asian Association for Regional Cooperation. Although there are major bilateral political differences and boundary disputes between the two major South Asian powers – India and Pakistan – the states of this region have so much in common that the creation of a sub-regional mechanism should be feasible.

The sixth is to update the Code of Manu – also known as the Code of Life or the Manusmriti – which was written by a Sanskrit scholar (most likely by a group of scholars under the leadership of sage Manu) around the 6th century BC. This is a work of genius, but it institutionalised the discriminatory caste system within Hinduism. The caste system has deeply troubled me for many years. There is a need for a modern version of the Manusmriti that incorporates modern principles of human rights. Having a national constitution that guarantees equality before the law and ratifying UN human rights treaties are ways to encourage reform. However, attempting to reform centuries-old beliefs is quite another matter. The discriminatory caste system is deeply rooted in the psyches of these traditional societies and the enactment of new political laws alone will not effect the desired change. Rather, laws must also be accompanied by the reform and modernisation of the scriptures. I would need to mobilise a large number of scholars within the Hindu world to accomplish this task.

The seventh is to revamp and transform the UN system of human rights to make it fit for the 21st century. I have already outlined my ideas for this in my book entitled *The Effectiveness of the UN Human Rights System.*[3] This is essentially my manifesto for a modern vision of the UN that would function better in today's multipolar world to help improve the lives of an ever increasing number of people around the globe.

The eighth is to contribute to the establishment of an international court of human rights through a new treaty or a protocol. I acknowledge that the judicialisation of international human rights alone will not bring human rights violations to an end, but the possibility of being found guilty through the binding decisions of an international human rights court, rather than a political body within the UN system, would deter many people in government and positions of authority from abusing their power, and afford more concrete legal remedies to the victims of human rights violations.

I hope I will have an opportunity to fulfil some of these dreams as I enter a phase of life described as 'yold' – somewhere between young and old. The fire in my belly is as strong as it was when I started my career in law. I have no fear of death; I fear only debilitating illness.

I regard myself as a Sherpa who has assisted eminent figures from the king of Nepal to the foreign secretary of the UK; confronted autocrats in countries such as Cambodia; and helped scholars and students alike from all over the world to scale the political and intellectual heights they have dreamed of. I am determined to continue assisting

3 Surya P. Subedi, *The Effectiveness of the UN Human Rights System* (London: Routledge, 2017).

people and institutions to help ensure that everybody on this planet can enjoy their human rights and fundamental freedoms in societies founded on the values of universalism, non-discrimination, tolerance, cohesion, and fraternity.

I consider myself a compassionate person – someone who notices suffering and acts to alleviate the pain. As a young man, I recognised the reality that political, social, and racial injustices cause tremendous pain; and that difficult times fall upon us all. While the suffering that each of us endures may be different, it is inevitable; it is part of our shared human experience. Recognising that pain, imperfections, and challenges are collective human experiences has led me to feel an inherent connectedness with people from all over the world. International law, I realised, has the potential to alleviate suffering. Thus, through my academic work, I have endeavoured to define, develop, and enhance this tool, which I have also applied to the best of my abilities in my many hands-on engagements to promote human rights.

And in my efforts to engender change, I have likewise adopted a compassionate approach, focused on preventing harmful behaviours rather than vilifying those responsible for them. I have found that the best results are obtained by securing the cooperation of the perpetrators in bringing about change for the better; persuading them to see the harmful impact of their actions on others; attending to those who have been harmed, and setting change in motion.

In his memoir, US President Bill Clinton wrote, 'Whether I'm a good man is, of course, for God to judge'[4] and I agree – it is for the gods to judge me. I would like to think that the young man who left his simple village in the hills of Nepal and ended up on a quest to promote democracy, the rule of law, and human rights both nationally and internationally has given his best both to the world and to his immediate and wider family. Being human, I have inevitably failed at times. No one leads a perfect or ideal life; rather, imperfections are part of our collective experience. I have always sought to learn from my failures, stay motivated, persevere, and try again. Failure can be our best teacher. Throughout my life, I have focused on how I can learn, grow, and develop in all situations – good and bad. Motivated by a deep sense of care, empathy, and compassion for people, I have strived to achieve the best possible outcomes.

4 Bill Clinton, *My Life* (New York: Hutchinson, 2004), p 4.

I believe in universalism – accepting all human beings as one family, respecting people's personal liberty and upholding liberal values in social interactions. This is in my blood, and hence I have done my best to lead my life as a global citizen and have encouraged my children, as well as my university students, to do likewise. While I have passed some milestones in life, the journey that I began in the hills of the Nepalese Himalayas many years ago continues to this day.

During my time as a visiting professor at the American University Washington College of Law in Washington, DC in 2012, I went to pay my respects to two distinguished American international lawyers, Judge Thomas Buergenthal and Judge Stephen Schwebel. They suggested that I had 30 years left ahead of me in which to achieve what I wanted to achieve in life. I do not know whether they knew my age – I was 54 at the time – but if I go by their advice, I have another 20 years to continue making a difference. And I will never tire in my efforts to do so.

Another towering intellectual figure based in Washington, DC, Mr Tom Veblen, jested that my life story would make a good novel, 'Who'd have ever guessed that a young fellow from Nepal would wind up in Oxford and go on to being recognized by the Queen as a significant contributor to making the United Kingdom a better place? That sounds more like a novel than a memoire'. Here is hoping that my story encourages readers to contribute to the protection of human rights and human dignity near and far.

Appendix

List of Publications by Professor Surya P. Subedi

Books

The Workings of Human Rights, Law and Justice: A Journey from Nepal to Nobel Nominee (Routledge, London/New York, 2022)

Human Rights in Eastern Civilisations: Some Reflections of a Former UN Special Rapporteur (Edward Elgar Publishing, Cheltenham, 2021)

Unilateral Sanctions in International Law (Hart Publishing, Oxford, 2021) (editor and lead author)

The Effectiveness of the UN Human Rights System: Reform and the Judicialization of Human Rights (Routledge, London/New York, 2017)

International Investment Law: Reconciling Policy and Principle (Hart Publishing, Oxford, 1st edition 2008; 2nd edition 2012; 3rd edition 2016; 4th edition 2020)

International Trade and Business Law (Hanoi Law University, Vietnam, 1st edition 2012; 2nd edition 2018) (edited as part of the EU-Vietnam Multilateral Trade Assistance Project (MUTRAP) III)

Dynamics of Foreign Policy and Law: A Study of Indo-Nepal Relations (Oxford University Press, New Delhi, 2005)

International Watercourses Law for the 21st Century: The Case of the River Ganges Basin (Ashgate Publishing, Aldershot, 2005) (editor and lead author)

Contemporary Issues in International Law: A Collection of the Josephine Onoh Memorial Lectures (edited with David Freestone and Scott Davidson) (Kluwer, The Hague/London, 2002)

Land and Maritime Zones of Peace in International Law (Oxford Monographs in International Law Series) (Clarendon: Oxford University Press, Oxford, 1996)

Land-Locked Nepal in International Law (K Gautam, Kathmandu, 1989)

Nepalese Administrative Law (Ratna Book Publishers, Kathmandu, 1st edition 1985; 2nd edition 1987; 3rd edition 1989) (in Nepali)

Scholarly Articles

'The Status of Dalit Women in Nepal', *Asian Yearbook of Human Rights and Humanitarian Law* (Vol VI), 2022

'Declaration on the Right to Development, 1986', *United Nations Audio Visual Library of International Law* (January 2021), https://legal.un.org/avl/ha/drd/drd.html, pp 1–9

'Changing Notions of Sovereignty and Governance of Water in India: An Analysis of the Inter-State Water Disputes Tribunal' (with A. Pandey), 26 *The Journal of Water Law* (2020), pp 167–181

'Responsibility to Protect and the International Military Intervention in Libya in International Law: What Went Wrong and What Lessons Could Be Learnt from It?' (with H. Teimouri), 23(1) *Journal of Conflict & Security Law* (Oxford University Press, Oxford, March 2018), pp 1–30

'Life as a UN Special Rapporteur: The Role of UN Special Rapporteurs in Developing International Law, the Impact of Their Work, and Some Reflections of the UN Special Rapporteur for Human Rights in Cambodia', 20 *Asian Yearbook of International Law* (2018), pp 12–52

'The Future of International Investment Regulation: Towards a World Investment Organisation?' (with Nicolette Butler), 64(1) *Netherlands International Law Review* (April 2017), pp 43–72

'The Disputes in the South China Sea and the United Nations Convention on the Law of the Sea', 14(1) *Soochow Law Journal* (January 2017), pp 15–41

'The UN Human Rights Special Rapporteurs and the Impact of Their Work: Some Reflections of the UN Special Rapporteur for Cambodia', 6(1) *Asian Journal of International Law* (Cambridge University Press, Cambridge, January 2016), pp 1–14

'The Universality of Human Rights and the UN Human Rights Agenda: The Impact of the Shift of Power to the East and the Resurgence of the BRICS', 55(2) *Indian Journal of International Law* (2015), pp 177–207

'China's Approach to Human Rights and the UN Human Rights Agenda', 14(3) *Chinese Journal of International Law* (Oxford University Press, Oxford, 2015), pp 437–464

'India's New Bilateral Investment Promotion and Protection Treaty with Nepal: A New Trend in State Practice', 28(2) *ICSID Review: Foreign Investment Law Journal* (Oxford University Press, Oxford, Fall 2013), pp384–404

'Land Rights in Countries in Transition: A Case Study of Human Rights Impact of Economic Land Concessions in Cambodia', 17 *Asian Yearbook of International Law* (2011), pp 1–46

'A Shift in Paradigm in International Economic Law: From State-Centric Principles to People-Centric Policies', 10(3) *Manchester Journal of International Economic Law* (2013), pp 314–335

'The WTO, Tuna and Dolphins: Has the Environment Lost Another Battle?' (with James Watson), 31 *Delhi Law Review* (2012) pp 21–43

'Problems and Prospects for the Commission on the Limits of the Continental Shelf in Dealing with Submissions by Coastal States in Relation to the Ocean Territory Beyond 200 Nautical Miles', 26 *International Journal of Marine and Coastal Law* (Martinus Nijhoff Publishers, The Hague, 2011), pp 413–431

'Protecting Human Rights through the Mechanism of UN Special Rapporteurs', 33 *Human Rights Quarterly* (2011), pp 201–228

'The UN Human Rights Mandate in Cambodia: The Challenges of a Country in Transition and the Experience of the UN Special Rapporteur for the Country', 15(2) *International Journal of Human Rights* (Taylor & Francis, London, 2011), pp 247–261

'Introduction: The Role of the Special Rapporteurs of the United Nations Human Rights Council in the Development and Promotion of International Human Rights Norms' (with Steven Wheatley et al), 15(2) *International Journal of Human Rights* (Taylor & Francis, London, 2011), pp 155–161

'Erosion of State Sovereignty under the Law of Foreign Investment: The Challenge of Balancing Investment Protection with the Sovereignty of Investment Receiving States', 6(1–4) *AALCO Quarterly Bulletin* (Asian-African Legal Consultative Organisation, New Delhi, 2010), pp 19–26

'The Notion of Free Trade and the First Ten Years of the World Trade Organization: How Level is the "Level Playing Field"?', 53(2) *Netherlands International Law Review* (Autumn 2006), pp 273–296

'The Challenge of Reconciling the Competing Principles within the Law of Foreign Investment with Special Reference to the Recent Trend in the Interpretation of the Term "Expropriation"', 40(1) *International Lawyer* (Spring 2006), pp 121–141

'The Legal Regime Concerning the Utilization of the Water Resources of the River Ganges Basin', 46 *German Yearbook of International Law* (2004), pp 452–493

'The Problems and Prospects of Offshore Banking in Nepal', 34(141) *Nyaydoot* (Nepal Bar Association, Kathmandu, English Special Issue, 2004), pp 1–8

'The Road from Doha: The Issues for the Development Round of the WTO and the Future of International Trade', 52(2) *International and Comparative Law Quarterly* (April 2003), pp 425–446

'The Concept in Hinduism of "Just War"', 8(2) *Journal of Conflict and Security Law* (Oxford University Press, Oxford, 2003), pp 339–361

'Developing the Disciplines of International Law and International Relations in Indonesian Higher Education', 2(3) *UNPAD Journal of International Law* (University of Padjadaran, Bandung, December 2003), pp 187–196

'The Himalayan Frontier Policy of British-India and the Significance of the 1923 Treaty of Friendship between Great Britain and Nepal', 27 *Journal of the Britain-Nepal Society* (December 2003), pp 35–39.

'The UN Response to International Terrorism in the Aftermath of the Terrorist Attacks in America and the Problem of the Definition of Terrorism in International Law', 4(3) *International Law FORUM du droit international: The Journal of the International Law Association* (August 2002), pp 158–168

'Regulation of Shared Water Resources in International Law: The Challenge of Balancing Competing Demands', 15(1 & 2) *Nepal Law Review* (Kathmandu, July 2002), pp 1–14

'Incorporation of the Principle of Sustainable Development into the Development Policies of the Asian Countries', 32(2) *Environmental Policy and Law* (International Council of Environmental Law, Bonn, April 2002), pp 85–90

'The UN Monterrey International Conference on Financing for Development', 4(2) *International Law FORUM du droit international: The Journal of the International Law Association* (May 2002), pp 52–53

'Hydro-Diplomacy in South Asia: The Conclusion of the Ganges and the Mahakali River Treaties', 93(4) *American Journal of International Law* (October 1999), pp 631–640

'Balancing International Trade with Environmental Protection: International Legal Aspects of Eco-Labels', 25(2) *Brooklyn Journal of International Law* (Fall 1999), pp 373–405

'Are the Principles of Human Rights "Western" Ideas? An Analysis of the Claim of the "Asian" Concept of Human Rights from the Perspectives of Hinduism', 30(1) *California Western International Law Journal* (Fall 1999), pp 45–69

'The Legal Competence of the International Community to Create "Safe Havens" in "Zones of Turmoil"', 12(1) *Journal of Refugee Studies* (Oxford University Press, March 1999), pp 23–35

'Constitutional Accommodation of Ethnicity and National Identity in Nepal', 6(1 & 2) *International Journal on Minority and Group Rights* (Kluwer Law International, The Hague, 1999), pp 121–147

'Problems and Prospects for the Treaty on the Creation of a Nuclear-Weapon-Free Zone in Southeast Asia', 4(1) *International Journal of Peace Studies* (January 1999), pp 63–78

'The Journey from an Oligarchy to a Parliamentary Democracy: A Case Study of Parliament in Nepal', 4(4) *The Journal of Legislative Studies* (London, Winter 1998), pp 163–182

'Environmental Inputs into the Planning Process and Access to Justice', 28(2) *Environmental Policy and Law* (May 1998), pp 96–103

'International Law and Land-Locked States: Development of the Freedom of Transit Prior to the Establishment of the United Nations,' serialised in *Nyayadoot* (Nepal Bar Association, Kathmandu), Vol 29, No 1, Issue 103 (pp 1–6), Vol 29, No 2, Issue 104 (pp 12–26) and Vol 29, No 3, Issue 105 (pp 16–24), 1998–99

'The United Nations and the Indian Ocean and the South Atlantic as Zones of Peace and Co-operation', 13 *Ocean Yearbook* (Chicago University Press, Chicago, 1998), pp 366–384

'Protection of Women against Domestic Violence: The Response of International Law', 2(6) *European Human Rights Law Review* (1997), pp 587–606

'Transit Arrangements between Nepal and India: A Study in International Law', 2(1) *Geopolitics and International Boundaries* (Frank Cass, London, 1997), pp 175–196

'When is a Treaty a Treaty in Law? An Analysis of the Views of the Supreme Court of Nepal on a Bilateral Water Agreement between Nepal and India', 5 *Asian Yearbook of International Law* (1996), pp 201–210

'The Common Foreign and Security Policy of the European Union and Neutrality: Towards Coexistence?', 42(3) *Netherlands International Law Review* (1995), pp 399–412

'The Doctrine of Objective Regimes in International Law and the Competence of the UN Security Council to Impose Territorial or Peace Settlements on States', 37 *German Yearbook of International Law* (1994), pp 162–205

'India-Nepal Security Relations and the 1950 Peace and Friendship Treaty: Time for New Perspectives', 34(3) *Asian Survey* (University of California Press, 1994), pp 273–284

'Neutrality in a Changing World: European Neutral States and the European Community', 42(2) *International and Comparative Law Quarterly* (March 1993), pp 238–268

'The Marine Fishery Rights of Land-Locked States with Particular Reference to the EEZ', 2(4) *International Journal of Marine and Coastal Law* (1987), pp 227–239

'Human Rights during Public Emergencies', *Obiter Dicta* (Hull University Law Students Journal, Hull), Vol 3, No 3, 1988, pp 25–31

Book Chapters

'Reconciling Public Interests with Private Interests in International Investment Arbitration and Securing Effective Remedy for Investment-Related Human Rights Violations', in Mahdev Mohan and Chester Brown (eds), *The Asian Turn in Foreign Investment* (Cambridge University Press, Cambridge, 2021), pp 363–378

'Enhancing State Responsibility from Environmental Implications of the South China Sea Dispute', (with Amrisha Pandey) in Richard Barnes and Ronan Long (eds), *Frontiers in International Environmental Law:*

Oceans and Climate Challenges: Essays in Honour of David Freestone (Martinus Nijhoff/Brill, The Hague, 2021), pp 339–367

'Nepal', in Simon Chesterman, Hisashi Owada and Ben Saul (eds), *The Oxford Handbook of International Law in Asia and the Pacific* (Oxford University Press, Oxford, 2019), pp 629–655 (with Pratyush Upreti)

'The Role of the Commission on the Outer Limits of the Continental Shelf in the Governance of the Seas and Oceans', in David Attard et al (eds), *The IMLI Treatise on Global Ocean Governance* (Vol 1: *UN and Global Ocean Governance*) (Oxford University Press, Oxford, 2018), pp 87–102

'International Investment Law', in Malcolm Evans (ed), *International Law* (5th edition, Oxford University Press, Oxford, 2018), pp 717–742

'The Art of Negotiating Investment Treaties and Investment Contracts in a Changing World of International Investment Law', in Americo B. Zampetti (ed), *Legal Assistance to Make Foreign Investment Work Better for Sustainable Development in the Least Developed Countries* (Occasional Policy Paper Series of the United Nations on the Least Developed Countries (No 2, 2017, United Nations, New York), pp 11–14

'Life as a UN Special Rapporteur: The Experience of the UN Special Rapporteur for Human Rights in Cambodia', in Aoife Nolan, Rosa Freedman and Therese Murphy (eds), *The United Nations Special Procedures System* (Brill/Martinus Nijhoff, Leiden/Boston, 2017), pp 297–314

'An Innovative Solution to an Ambitious Project: Dispute Resolution in the 1982 Convention on the Law of the Sea', in Charles C. Jalloh and Olufemi Elias (eds), *Shielding Humanity: Essays in International Law in Honour of Judge Abdul G Koroma* (Martinus Nijhoff/Brill, The Hague, 2015), pp 163–186

'International Law Response to Land Grabbing in Asia', in Connie Carter and Andrew Harding (eds), *Land Grabs in Asia: What Role for the Law?* (Routledge, Abingdon, 2015), pp 24–34

'Human Rights Experts in the United Nations: A Review of the Role of the United Nations Special Procedures', in Monika Ambrus et al (eds), *The Role of 'Experts' in International and European Decision-Making Process* (Cambridge University Press, Cambridge, 2014), pp 241–262

'International Investment Law', in Malcolm Evans (ed), *International Law* (4th edition, Oxford University Press, Oxford, 2014), pp 727–751

'Human Rights and Economic Land Concessions: A Study of Cambodia', in Jo Carby-Hall (ed), *Essays on Human Rights* (Ius et Lex Foundation, Warsaw, 2014), pp 450–466

'Commission on Sustainable Development', in Rudiger Wolfrum (ed), *The Max Planck Encyclopaedia of Public International Law* (Oxford University Press, Oxford, 2012), Vol II, pp 418–422

'Ganges River', in Rudiger Wolfrum (ed), *The Max Planck Encyclopaedia of Public International Law* (Oxford University Press, Oxford, 2012), Vol IV, pp 288–292

'Indus River', in Rudiger Wolfrum (ed), *The Max Planck Encyclopaedia of Public International Law* (Oxford University Press, Oxford, 2012), Vol V, pp 157–160

'Nepal', in Rudiger Wolfrum (ed), *The Max Planck Encyclopaedia of Public International Law* (Oxford University Press, Oxford, 2012), Vol VII, pp 606–612

'WTO Dispute Settlement Mechanism as a New Technique for Settling Disputes in International Law', in Duncan French, Matthew Saul and Nigel D. White (eds), *International Law and Dispute Settlement: New Problems and Techniques* (Hart Publishing, Oxford, 2010), pp 173–190

'Reassessing and Redefining the Principle of Economic Sovereignty of States', in Duncan French (ed), *Global Justice and Sustainable Development* (Brill, The Hague, 2010), pp 403–410

'Post-Conflict Constitutional Settlement in Nepal and the Role of the United Nations', in Morly Frishman and Sam Muller (eds), *The Dynamics of Constitutionalism in the Age of Globalisation* (Hague Academic Press, The Hague, 2010), pp 71–87

'The Challenges to the National Security of Nepal and the Role of International Law and Foreign Policy', in Rajan Bhattarai and Geja S. Wagle (eds), *Emerging Security Challenges of Nepal* (Nepal Institute for Policy Studies, Kathmandu, 2010), pp 65–110

'The Challenge of Reconciling Competing Interests in the Law of Foreign Investment', in Mary George et al (eds), *The Place of International Obligations in the Domestic Legal Order of States* (Institute of Ocean and Earth Sciences, University of Malaya, Kuala Lumpur, 2008), pp 95–105

'Access to Environmental Justice in a Politically Unstable Environment: A Case Study of Nepal', in Andrew Harding (ed), *Access to Environmental Justice: A Comparative Study* (Brill/Martinus Nijhoff, The Hague, 2007), pp 157–176

'The Status of International Humanitarian Law in Nepal' (with Hari Phuyal), in V.S. Mani (ed), *Handbook of International Humanitarian Law in South Asia* (Oxford University Press, New Delhi, 2007), pp 86–91

'The Challenges Ahead for the World Bank and the International Monetary Fund with Regard to the Human Rights Agenda', in C. Raj Kumar and D.K. Srivastava (eds), *Human Rights and Development: Law, Policy and Governance* (LexisNexis, Butterworths, Hong Kong/Singapore/Malaysia in association with City University of Hong Kong, 2006), pp 177–188

'Property Rights of Women in Nepal' (with Ila Sharma), in Diane Ryland (ed), *An Era of Human Rights: International Legal Essays in Honour of Professor Jo Carby-Hall* (Barmarick Publications, Patrington, 2006), pp 447–457

'The War on Terror and U.N. Attempts to Adopt a Comprehensive Convention on International Terrorism', in Paul Eden and Therese O'Donnell (eds), *September 11, 2001: A Turning Point in International and Domestic Law?* (Transnational Publishers, Inc, New York, 2005), pp 207–225

'Regulation of Shared Water Resources in International Law: The Challenge of Balancing Competing Demands in International Law', in Surya P. Subedi (ed), *International Watercourses Law for the 21st Century: The Case of the River Ganges Basin* (Ashgate Publishing, Aldershot, 2005), pp 7–18 (republished)

'The Challenge of Managing the "Second Agricultural Revolution" through International Law: Liberalization of Trade in Agriculture and Sustainable Development', in Nico Schrijver and Friedl Weiss (eds), *International Law and Sustainable Development: Principles and Practice* (Martinus Nijhoff, The Hague, 2004), pp 161–184

'Decisions of National Tribunals Concerning International Environmental Law: Cases Decided by the Supreme Court of Nepal', *International Environmental Law Reports* (Cambridge University Press, Cambridge), Vol 4, 2004, pp 321–329

'Regulation of Foreign Investment and the Development Round of the WTO', in Kim van der Borght et al (eds), *Essays on the Future of the WTO: Finding a New Balance* (Cameron May, London, 2003), pp 87–103

'Multinational Corporations and Human Rights', in Karin Arts and Paschal Miyho (eds), *Responding to the Human Rights Deficit* (Kluwer Law International, The Hague, 2003), pp 171–184

'Resolution of International Water Disputes: Challenges for the 21st Century', in *International Bureau of the Permanent Court of Arbitration, Resolution of International Water Disputes* (Volume 6 in the PCA Peace Palace Papers series, Kluwer Law International, The Hague, 2003), pp 33–47

'Sustainable Development Perspectives in International Economic Law', in Asif H. Qureshi (ed), *Perspectives in International Economic Law* (Kluwer Law International Law, The Hague, 2002), pp 261–276

'International Legal Aspects of Eco-Labels', in Michael Bothe and Peter H. Sand (eds), *Environmental Policy from Regulation to Economic Instruments* (The Hague Academy of International Law, Martinus Nijhoff, The Hague, 2002), pp 191–218 (republished)

'Foreign Investment and Sustainable Development', in Friedl Weiss et al (eds), *Towards International Economic Law with a Human Face* (Kluwer Law International, The Hague, 1998), pp 413–428

'The United Nations and the Trade and Transit Problems of Land-Locked States', in Martin Glassner (ed), *The United Nations at Work* (Greenwood Publishing, Inc., Westport, 1998), pp 134–160

'The Foreign Policy of the European Union and Asian States: Views from Beyond the European Union', in Wybo P. Here (ed), *Contemporary International Law Issues: New Forms, New Applications* (TMC Asser Institute, The Hague, 1998), pp 235–238

'Indo-Nepal Relations: The Causes of Conflict and their Resolution', in Subrata K. Mitra and Dietmar Rothermund (eds), *Legitimacy and Conflict in South Asia* (New Delhi Branch of Heidelberg University & Manohar, New Delhi/Heidelberg, 1997), pp 220–245.

'The Right of Self-Determination and Tibetan People', in Dino Kritsiotis (ed), *Self-Determination: Cases of Crisis* (University of Hull Law School, Hull, 1994), pp 1–16.

'Comments on Humanitarian Intervention in International Law', in Holly Cullen et al (eds), *Politics and Law of Former Yugoslavia* (University of Hull European Community Research Unit, Hull, 1993), pp 70–72

Published Reports

'The Situation of Human Rights in Cambodia in 2014', Sixth Report (final and concluding report) to the UN Human Rights Council in August 2014 (UN Doc A/HRC/27/70) as the UN Special Rapporteur for Human Rights in Cambodia

'The Situation of Human Rights in Cambodia in 2013', Fifth Report to the UN Human Rights Council in September 2013 (UN Doc A/HRC/24/36) as the UN Special Rapporteur for Human Rights in Cambodia

'A Human Rights Analysis of Economic and other Land Concessions in Cambodia' as the UN Special Rapporteur for Human Rights in Cambodia and published by the United Nations Office of the High Commissioner for Human Rights, Geneva in September 2012 (UN Doc A/HRC/21/63/Add1)

'The Situation of Human Rights in Cambodia in 2012', Fourth Report (focused on electoral reform) to the UN Human Rights Council in September 2012 (UN Doc A/HRC/21/63) as the UN Special Rapporteur for Human Rights in Cambodia

'The Situation of Human Rights in Cambodia in 2011', Third Report (focused on parliamentary reform) to the UN Human Rights Council in September 2011 (UN Doc A/HRC/18/46) as the UN Special Rapporteur for Human Rights in Cambodia

'The Situation of Human Rights in Cambodia in 2010', Second Report (focused on judicial reform) to the UN Human Rights Council in September 2010 (UN Doc A/HRC/15/46) as the UN Special Rapporteur for Human Rights in Cambodia

'The Situation of Human Rights in Cambodia in 2009', First Report (the general situation of human rights situation in the country) to the UN Human Rights Council in August 2009 (UN Doc A/HRC/12/40) as the UN Special Rapporteur for Human Rights in Cambodia

'Development of a Legal Framework for Co-operation among India, Nepal and Bangladesh on the Management of the Water Resources of the River Ganges Basin' (with Professor BS Chimni) to the Dutch Research Council WOTRO under the Indo-Dutch Programme on Alternatives in Development, The Hague, 2002, p 150

'A Review of Marine and Coastal Environmental Protection Legislation' (with S. Read, M. Elliott and D. Symes) to WWF-UK, the Wildlife Trusts and the Institute of Estuarine and Coastal Studies, University of Hull, 2000, p 108

Books Edited in the Routledge Series on 'Human Rights and International Law'

The Presumption of Innocence in International Human Rights and Criminal Law (Routledge Publishing, London/New York, 2021) by Michelle Coleman

Human Rights, Religion and International Law (Routledge Publishing, London/New York, 2020) by Kerry O'Halloran

Sexual Orientation, Gender Identity and International Human Rights Law: Common Law Perspectives (Routledge Publishing, London/New York, 2019) by Kerry O'Halloran

The Right to the Truth in International Law: Victims' Rights in Human Rights and International Criminal Law (Routledge Publishing, London/New York, 2019) by Melanie Klinkner and Howard Davis

Extracting Accountability from Non-State Actors in International Law: Assessing the Scope for Direct Regulation (Routledge Publishing, London/New York, 2018) by Lee James McConnell

The Emerging Law of Forced Displacement in Africa: Development and Implementation of the Kampala Convention on Internal Displacement (Routledge Publishing, London/New York, 2018) by Allehone M. Abebe

The Legal Protection of Women from Violence: Normative Gaps in International Law (Routledge Publishing, London/New York, 2016) by Rashida Manjoo and Jackie Jones

Tax Havens and International Human Rights (Routledge Publishing, London/New York, 2017) by Paul Beckett

Socio-Economic Human Rights in Essential Public Services Provision (Routledge Publishing, London/New York, 2016) by Marlies Hesselman, Antenor Hallo de Wolf and Brigit Toebes

Business and Human Rights: History, Law and Policy – Bridging the Accountability Gap (Routledge Publishing, London/New York, 2016) by Nadia Bernaz
Human Rights and Development in International Law (Routledge Publishing, London/New York, 2016) by Tahmina Karimova
Human Rights and Charity Law: International Perspectives (Routledge Publishing, London/New York, 2016) by Kerry O'Halloran

Other Publications as Editor or Chief Editor

Founding Executive Editor between 2010 and 2015 and Chief Editor since 2015 of the *Asian Journal of International Law* (Cambridge University Press)
General (Chief) Editor between 1999 and 2006 of the *Asian Yearbook of International Law* (Martinus Nijhoff, The Hague)

Select Shorter Articles

'What is Missing in Nepal', *CNN*, 28 April 2015, www.cnn.com/2015/04/28/opinions/subedi-nepal-earthquake/index.html
'Secularism in Hinduism', *The Kathmandu Post*, 1 June 2006, p 4
'Restoring Democracy: Taming the King of Nepal', *The International Herald Tribune*, 4 June 2005, p 6
'OBE Acceptance Speech', *Newsletter of the International Law Association*, No 22, 2005, London, pp 10–12
'Introduction', *International Law and Imperialism*, by Professor Martti Koskenniemi, University of Hull Law School in Studies in Law Series 1999
'Introduction', *Beyond Kosovo: The United Nations and Humanitarian Intervention*, by Dr Ralph Zacklin, Assistant Secretary-General for Legal Affairs of the United Nations, University of Hull Law School in Studies in Law Series 2000

Book Reviews

'Behind the Killing Fields: A Khmer Rouge Leader and One of His Victims' by Gina Chon and Sambeth Thet, 33(3) *Human Rights Quarterly* (August 2011), pp 878–879
'The Expropriation of Environmental Governance: Protecting Foreign Investors at the Expense of Public Policy' (with Nicolette Butler) by Kyla Tienhaara, 4 *Journal of World Energy Law and Business* (Oxford University Press, Oxford, 2011), pp 201–203
'Fresh Water and International Economic Law' by EB Weiss et al (eds), 77 *British Yearbook of International Law* (2006), pp 453–454

'Ecological Sensitivity and Global Legal Pluralism: Rethinking the Trade and Environment Conflict' by Oren Perez, 76 *British Yearbook of International Law* (2005), pp 351–352

'The Law of International Watercourses: Non-Navigational Uses' by Stephen McCaffrey, 73 *British Yearbook of International Law* (2002), pp 375–376

'The Razor's Edge: International Boundaries and Political Geography', by Clive Schofield et al (eds), 9 *Asian Yearbook of International Law* (2004), pp 426–427

'The Political Economy of International Trade Law: Essays in Honour of Robert E. Hudec' by Daniel L.M. Kennedy and James D. Southwick (eds), *Lloyd's Maritime and Commercial Law Quarterly* (2003), pp 549–550

'Transnational Environmental Law: Lessons in Global Change' by Peter H. Sand (Kluwer Law International, The Hague, 1999), 8 *Asian Yearbook of International Law* (2003), pp 332–333

'International Monetary Law: Issues for the New Millennium' by Marion Giovanoli, 117 *The Law Quarterly Review* (Sweet & Maxwell, 2001), pp 176–178

'Regional Peacekeeping in the Post-Cold War Era' by Hilaire McCoubrey and Justin Morris, 50 *International and Comparative Law Quarterly* (January 2001), pp 207–208

'Yearbook of International Co-operation on Environment and Development' by Helge Ole Bergesen et al (eds), 2(4) *Environmental Law Review* (2000), p 303

'The Law of Non-Navigational Uses of International Watercourses' by J. Bruhacs, 7 *Asian Yearbook of International Law* (2001), pp 496–497

'Multinational Enterprises and the Law' by Peter Muchlinski, 7 *Asian Yearbook of International Law* (2001), pp 495–496

'Modern Indian Family Law' by Werner F. Menski, 65(2) *Bulletin of the School of Oriental and African Studies* (University of London, 2002), pp 379 ff

'International Law Studies: Collected Papers' (Volume II) by Anthony D'Amato, 47(2) *International and Comparative Law Quarterly* (April 1998), p 475

'Recognition of Governments: Legal Doctrine and State Practice, 1815–1995' by M.J. Peterson, 47 *Political Studies* (March 1999), pp 203 ff

'Manual of European Environmental Law' (2nd edition) by Alexandre Kiss and Dinah Shelton, 29(3) *Law Librarian* (September 1998), pp 187–188

'Human Rights Approaches to Environmental Protection' by Alan E. Boyle and Michael Anderson (eds), 9(2) *African Journal of International and Comparative Law* (June 1997), pp 534–536

'The Legal Regulation of the European Community's External Relations after the Completion of the Internal Market' by Stratos V. Konstadinidis (ed), 3(2) *European Public Law* (June 1997), pp 291–293

'The Legal Regime for Transboundary Water Pollution: Between Discretion and Constraint' by Andre Nollkaemper, *International Journal of Marine and Coastal Law* (1996), 11, pp 416–418

'The International Law on Foreign Investment' by M. Sornarajah, 6 *Asian Yearbook of International Law* (1996), pp 476–477

'Water and the Quest for Sustainable Development in the Ganges Valley' by G.P. Chapman and M. Thompson (eds), 27(4) *Development and Change* (October 1996), pp 821–822

'United Nations and the Gulf Crisis' by R.P. Anand, 5 *Asian Yearbook of International Law* (1995), pp 516–517

'The Future of the International Nuclear Non-Proliferation Regime' by Marianne van Leeuwen (ed), 49(7/8) *International Spectator* (1995), pp 426–427 (in Dutch)

'Fundamental Rights in Sri Lanka: A Commentary' by S. Sharvananda, 5 *Asian Yearbook of International Law* (1995), pp 513–515

'Foreign Aid, Poverty and Stagnation in Nepal' by Narayan Khadka, 2(2) *Contemporary South Asia* (Oxford, 1993), pp 220–221

Index

Note: Page numbers in *italics* indicate figures, and references following "n" refer endnotes.

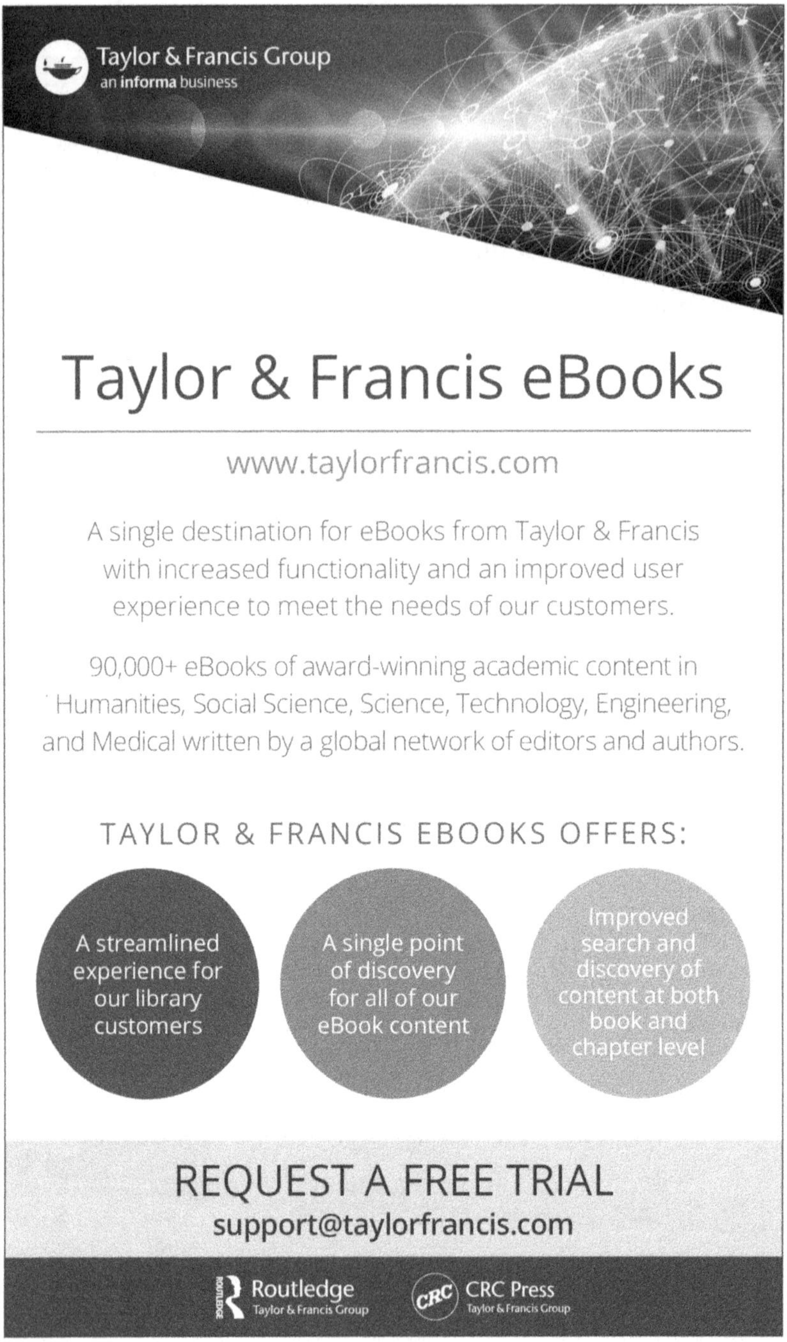
Taylor & Francis Group
an informa business
Taylor & Francis eBooks
www.taylorfrancis.com
A single destination for eBooks from Taylor & Francis with increased functionality and an improved user experience to meet the needs of our customers.
90,000+ eBooks of award-winning academic content in Humanities, Social Science, Science, Technology, Engineering, and Medical written by a global network of editors and authors.
TAYLOR & FRANCIS EBOOKS OFFERS:
A streamlined experience for our library customers
A single point of discovery for all of our eBook content
Improved search and discovery of content at both book and chapter level
REQUEST A FREE TRIAL
support@taylorfrancis.com
Routledge
Taylor & Francis Group
CRC Press
Taylor & Francis Group

For Product Safety Concerns and Information please contact our EU representative GPSR@taylorandfrancis.com
Taylor & Francis Verlag GmbH, Kaufingerstraße 24, 80331 München, Germany

www.ingramcontent.com/pod-product-compliance
Lightning Source LLC
LaVergne TN
LVHW021127300926
849160LV00010B/901

* 9 7 8 1 0 3 2 2 2 2 0 3 5 *